2004 P...

ONCE UPON A RHYME

IMAGINATION FOR
A NEW GENERATION

Poems From
Northern England
Edited by Steve Twelvetree

Happy 75ᵗʰ birthday

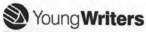

Young**Writers**

First published in Great Britain in 2005 by:
Young Writers
Remus House
Coltsfoot Drive
Peterborough
PE2 9JX
Telephone: 01733 890066
Website: www.youngwriters.co.uk

SB ISBN 1 84460 670 8

Foreword

Young Writers was established in 1991 and has been passionately devoted to the promotion of reading and writing in children and young adults ever since. The quest continues today. Young Writers remains as committed to engendering the fostering of burgeoning poetic and literary talent as ever.

This year's Young Writers competition has proven as vibrant and dynamic as ever and we are delighted to present a showcase of the best poetry from across the UK. Each poem has been carefully selected from a wealth of *Once Upon A Rhyme* entries before ultimately being published in this, our twelfth primary school poetry series.

Once again, we have been supremely impressed by the overall high quality of the entries we have received. The imagination, energy and creativity which has gone into each young writer's entry made choosing the best poems a challenging and often difficult but ultimately hugely rewarding task - the general high standard of the work submitted amply vindicating this opportunity to bring their poetry to a larger appreciative audience.

We sincerely hope you are pleased with our final selection and that you will enjoy *Once Upon A Rhyme Poems From Northern England* for many years to come.

Contents

Ryan Marley (10)   20
Robert Bland (10)   21
Amy Laverick (9)   21
Emily Gibson (10)   22
Ben Snaith (10)   22
Rebecca Bastiman (10)   23
John Hagan (9)   23
Jon Iseton (9)   23
Kenneth Woodier (10)   24
Scott Jones (10)   24
Alexandra Brady (10)   24
Jessica Smith (10)   25
Laura McMenamin (10)   25
Andrew Berry (9)   25
Thomas Arnold (9)   26
Megan Williams (9)   26
Jamie Lee Wells (9)   26

Hutton Rudby Primary School, Hutton Rudby

Sam Gunn (9)   27
Sarah McAsey (9)   27
Becky Devereux (9)   28
Rachael Boyle (9)   28
Mark Artley (9)   29
Sebastian Langston (9)   29
Jacob Straw (10)   30
Harriet Atkinson (9)   30
Harry Kitching (9)   31
Jack Martin Williamson (9)   31
Sophie Victoria Robinson (9)   32
Aidan Broadhurst (9)   32
William Loader (10)   33
Matthew Hodgson (9)   33
Christopher Loader (10)   34
Alexander Rogers (9)   34
Philip Hutchinson (9)   34
Elena Leyshon (9)   35
Craig Lockyer (10)   35
Bethany Brown (9)   36
Bruce Hall (9)   36
Georgia E J Slade (9)   37

Linthorpe Community Primary School, Middlesbrough

Emily Wheatley (10)	54
Jack Burns (10)	54
Zeeshan Mehmood (10)	55
Hayley Harrowsmith (10)	55
Nyla Akhtar (10)	56
Michael Edon (10)	56
Katie Thompson (7)	57
Perry Morgan (10)	57
Charlotte Jones (8)	58
Hannah Scott (7)	58
Lucy McCall (8)	58
Amy Glazebrook (9)	59
Joshua Young (8)	59
Kaleem Majid (8)	59
Laura Foster (8)	60
Kennedy Smith Cassy (8)	60
Saffron Bowyer-Hogg (10)	60
Sara Cooper (10)	61
Joshua Cassidy (10)	61
Megan McCullow (11)	62
Faisal Hussain (11)	62
Hayley McFarlane (10)	63
Ryonni Daggett (10)	63
Philip James (10)	64
Richard Cowley (10)	64
Jack Boocock (11)	65
Katie Dixon (10)	65
Chloe Jones (10)	66
Emma Hall (10)	66
Elena Durrani (10)	67
Emily Hood (10)	67
Daniel Smith (10)	67
Robert Ellis (10)	68
Anthony Snook (10)	68
Andrew North (10)	68
Lateef Owarth (10)	69
Scott David Rogers (10)	69
Elizabeth Devereux (11)	70
Faye Moore (10)	70
Helena Hussain (10)	70
Amy Dixon (10)	71
Sayeed Hussain Buksh (10)	71

Paige Elizabeth Ferguson (10)   72
Charlotte Stoddart (10)   72
Jasmine Thomas (9)   72
Samaira Riaz (10)   73
Marie Brown (11)   73
Thalia Bloundele (10)   74
Imogen Ord-Smith (10)   74
Jordan Cane (10)   74
Lauren Boden (11)   75
Stefan Dezou (9)   75
Lee Maskew (10)   75
Christopher Larkman (10)   76
Olivia Hood (10)   76

Marton Grove Primary School, Middlesbrough

Amey Sanders   77
Sophie Jinks (10)   77
Lauren Wilson (10)   77
Emma Clare (10)   78
Harry William Drake (10)   78
Kelsey Morris (10)   78
Connor Richardson (10)   79
Lewis Paul Thompson (10)   79
Sophie Batey (10)   79
Daniel Chirnside (10)   80
Jade Frost (11)   80
Lewis Wigham (10)   80
Robert Daniel Harman (10)   81

Priory Woods Special School, Middlesbrough

Faisal Mohammed, Christopher Dillon, Akbar Arshad (11),
    Sean Laver, Sophie Spence & Kirsty Veitch (12)   81

St Clare's RC Primary School, Acklam

Jessica Seale (8)   82
Dominic Ragusa (10)   82
Tessa Molly Anna Stobbs (8)   83
Stephen Connors (8)   84
Taylor Middleton (9)   84
Kathryn Clarke (8)   85
Luke Symmonds (8)   85

Moly Sherwood (8)	86
Luciano Rossi (9)	86
Josh Hutchinson (8)	87
Oliver Hughes (8)	87
Jordan Hood (8)	88
Hannah Crackell (8)	88
Katie White (8)	89
Jonathan James Coleby (9)	90
Emily Callaghan (9)	90
Nicole Richmond (8)	91
Nicole Pritchard (8)	91
Helen Kathleen Kuby (8)	92
Hayley Nicholas (8)	93
Daniel Hyde (9)	93
Jacy Yates (8)	94
Sarah Connor (8)	95
Lucy McElhone (8)	96
Sarah Louise Price (9)	97
Jade McElwee (9)	97
Katy McHugh (9)	98
Beth Knight (9)	99
Sarah Mitchell (9)	99
Chloe Meehan (9)	100
Jenny Linsley (9)	101
Peter F Martin (10)	102
Richard John Martin (9)	102
Ellie Clarke (10)	103
Ross Young (9)	104
Luke Allen (10)	105
Harriet Glence (9)	105
Michael James Bythway (9)	106
Kate Hilton (9)	107
Tom Driscoll (9)	108
Deanna Parry (9)	109
Charlie Collin (9)	109
Luke Bollands (9)	110
Louis Stobbs (9)	110
Chloe Tempestoso (9)	111
Jessica McKinley (9)	112

St Mark's Elm Tree Primary School, Fairfield

Sarah Pinkney (11)	112
Ryan Todd (10)	113
Charlotte McCann (10)	113
Rachel Hartley (10)	114
Lauren Rodgers (10)	115
Christopher Scott (10)	115
Daniel Boston (11)	116
Phillip Rowe (9)	116
Claire Stephenson (10)	116
Bethany Riley (10)	117
Rebecca Moira Bean (10)	117
Ryan Morgan (11)	118
Ryan Harwood (11)	118
Cara Barugh (10)	119
Ryan Bennett (10)	119
Alexander Kitching (10)	120
Adam Melville (8)	120
Amy Pickard (9)	121
Jack Rutter (10)	121
Beth Cash (9)	122
Megan Bullas (9)	122
Jade Taylor (9)	123
Sophie Clarkson (9)	123
Laura Hood (9)	124
Joshua Phipps (7)	124
Paige Young (9)	125
Abbie Stoddart (8)	125
Rebecca Alexander & Emily Robinson (9)	126
Emma Armstrong (7)	126
Harry Teasdale (9)	127
Abbie Wilkinson (9)	127
Alun Littlefair (9)	128
Nicholas Williams (9)	128
Lucas Connor (7)	129
Oliver Riddle (9)	129
Mark Hill (9)	129
Kirsty Harrison (10)	130

Teesside Preparatory & High School, Eaglescliffe

William Cassidi CE Primary School, Stillington

Adam James Glass (9)	147
Christopher Taylor (7)	148
Thomas Liam Holdsworth (7)	148
Daniel Butler (7)	148
Eliot Barley (9)	149
Adam Wells (9)	149
Chloe Bloomfield (9)	149
Ioannis Daniel Kolios (8)	150
Liam Osborne (8)	150
Nicholas Abrahams (7)	150
Gayle Tait (10)	151
Andrew Hawes (7)	151
Fleur Durham (8)	151
Grace Maloney (7)	152
William King (7)	152
Oliver Bell (7)	152
Alexandra Cornelius (9)	153
Eleanor Smith (9)	153
Holly Armstrong (10)	153
Rebecca Drew (10)	154
Alice Constantine (10)	154
Ben Wells (9)	154
Lewis Cotts (9)	155
Mathew Robinson (9)	155
Kate Wilkinson (9)	155
Rachael Ross (9)	156
Paul Ruddle (9)	156
Isaac Allen (7)	156
Hannah Norman (9)	157
Olivia Durham (9)	157
Dale Howe (9)	158
Christopher Michael Holdsworth (9)	158
Elliot Sharp (9)	159
Chris Holmes (9)	159
Helen French (9)	160
Luke Johnson (9)	160

Yarm CP School, Yarm

Olivia McLurg (9)	161
Anand Krishna (8)	161
Kate Chapman (9)	162

Kimberley Foster (11)	182
William Levitt (8)	183
Alistair Aitken (10)	183
Hannah Sayer (10)	184
Helen Probert (8)	184
Evie Thompson (10)	185
Emily Rankin (8)	185
Ellie Bourner (8)	186
Rowan Bliss (9)	186
Charlotte Cooney (9)	187
Curtis Mackay (10)	187
Sally Leishman (9)	188
Joseph Rodgers (8)	188
Sophie Bell (9)	189
Matthew Healey (8)	189
Jack Chapman (10)	190
Eloise Crofts (10)	190
Alexander Murray (10)	191
Luke Bourner (10)	191
Amélie Cowan (10)	192
Sean Brown (8)	192
Adam Herbert (8)	193
Harry Spencer (8)	193
Oliver Dryden (8)	193
Josephine Welsh (10)	194
Jacob Stokes (8)	194
Matthew Nargol (8)	194
Jason Barnes (10)	195
Tom Elliott (10)	195
Bethany Gray (11)	196
Lauren Jackson (11)	197
Oliver Campbell (10)	197
Siân Gers (10)	198
Tim Spencer (10)	198
Emily Hadlow (10)	199
Benjamin Andrews (10)	200
Jonathan Colclough (10)	200
Sophie Cullum (10)	201
James Heavers (10)	201
James Harkin (10)	202
Harry Robinson (10)	202
Samantha Wilkin (10)	203

The Poems

A Gentle Breeze

The water trickles slowly
Like a lethargic dripping tap,
On windowpanes and doors and roofs,
So heavy it may snap.
But the wind is blowing gently
Like a leaf inside a maze,
And the fish swim in the river
And the cows are out to graze.
The birds are on the branches
In their cosy little nest,
The dogs are in their kennels
As the wind blows from the west.

The river's overflowing
Like a gushing waterfall,
On upturned umbrellas
Of the stormy evening's call.
The streets are getting colder
And the fog starts to appear,
The phones are dead and nothing's said,
The hurricane is near.

Laura Stuart (10)
Acklam Whin Primary School, Middlesbrough

The Happy And The Sad

Happiness is opening
Like a warming sunrise
On the land and the hills and the sea
And then the sun dies.
But the moon is still alive
Like a gleaming, silver ball
And the stars act as his guide
Like a giraffe, standing tall.
But the badger's very sad
Like a crying cloud of rain
And the lost baby bird
Is like a child with no name.

Laliesha Ali (10)
Acklam Whin Primary School, Middlesbrough

As . . .

As white as my mum's glittering wedding gown
and as black as a witch's long, dangling cloak.

As light as a drifting little feather and as heavy as the universe.

As happy as a child on their birthday
and as sad as an orphan seeing their mum taken away.

As slow as a tortoise in a race
and as fast as a cheetah going its normal pace.

As full as my tummy, big and bursting
and as empty as a Cadbury's chocolate box.

As hot as water in my boiling bath
and as cold as cold ice from the Antarctic.

As free as the stars in the moonlit sky
and as trapped as a prisoner in his mind . . .

Jodie Flynn (11)
Bader Primary School, Thornaby

My Coloured Paintbrush

Red is a sign of danger,
Blood on a sword,
The glowing eyes of foxes,
Boro kit staying red.

Black is the colour of sky,
A sign of rain,
The opposite of white,
Another dull colour.

Gold is the World Cup,
A shooting star,
A death mask,
The colour of delight.

Green is the grass in springtime,
A colour that stands out,
Bushes with nettles,
A colour for safety.

Blue is for cold,
But also for fun,
A colour that represents water,
The colour of veins.

Charlie Raby (9)
Bader Primary School, Thornaby

My Paintbox

Blue is an icy, cold colour,
A dark blue stream,
A sapphire gleam in the sun,
Water trickling from a tap.

Gold is a star glistening at night,
The moon shining on the ground,
A coin glistening in the sunlight,
The Queen's precious crown.

Green is luscious grass at springtime,
A cat's eyes glowing in the dark,
A frog swimming in the river,
A snake slithering in the jungle.

Red is a rosy apple hanging off a tree,
A ruby sparkling in the sunshine,
Foxes eyes glowing at night,
A clown's nose squirting water out.

Black is a scary colour,
A haunted house,
A stormy cloud filled with heavy rain,
A shadow following you at night.

Jessica Nowell (9)
Bader Primary School, Thornaby

My Paintbox

Red is a rose smelling sweet as can be,
A rosy-red apple falling from a tree,
The fiery flames from a dragon,
A ruby gem shining in the sun.

Green is grass in springtime,
An emerald as green as can be,
Sour lime getting poured into a cup,
A straight stem on a flower.

Black is a stormy night sky,
A haunted house scarier than anything,
A shadow following you at night,
A black cloud filled with heavy rain.

Gold is a star shining in the sky,
A sheriff's badge for all his bravery,
Some corn swaying in the wind,
Tutunkhamun's death mask gleaming.

Blue is a summer sky,
The sea reflecting in the sky,
A tap dripping very slowly,
The River Nile wandering through the desert.

Chloe Hopson (9)
Bader Primary School, Thornaby

My Paintbox Colours

Red is a ruby getting stolen,
A sweet-smelling rose showing in the grass,
Fire roaring of a dragon's mouth
Sunset in the sky.

Black is a shadow on the brick wall,
Mysterious magic filling the crowded streets,
Fumes of cars giving people chances of dying,
Haunted houses spooking people out of their wits.

Green is the fresh grass,
Fully grown frogs jumping from lily pad to lily pad,
Poisonous chemicals dumped into rivers,
Cats' eyes glowing in the dark.

Blue is the colour of your veins,
People turning blue by freezing to death,
Summer sky reflecting against the sea,
Fish swimming in the blue water.

Gold is a flying star glistening in the sky,
The Queen's rare crown sparkling in the window,
Diamonds reflecting on the gold cushion,
Corn waving in the wind.

Natasha Lackenby (9)
Bader Primary School, Thornaby

Colours In My Paintbox

Gold is the Queen's precious crown,
A shooting star zooming past our houses,
A coin glittering in the sun,
Hidden treasure in a pyramid.

Red is the sign of danger,
A beautiful sunset at the end of the day,
The fiery flames of a fire,
The blood dripping from a sword.

Blue is a wintry colour,
The icicles hanging from the roof,
The lovely, deep sea,
A sapphire glittering in the sun.

Green is a cat's eyes glowing in the dark,
Or a lovely apple about to fall off a tree,
The luscious, green grass,
A lovely emerald glittering in the light.

Black is a robber running in the night,
A dark, gloomy house,
A storm cloud filled with rain,
The dark night sky.

Bethany Fleming (9)
Bader Primary School, Thornaby

The Colours In My Box

Black is a stormy sky,
A haunted house,
A dark shadow at night
And horrible, mysterious magic.

Red is a ruby-red gem sparkling in the sunset,
A rosy-red apple falling from a tree,
And glowing red eye like a fox's tail,
A dragon's red-hot flame like a volcano.

Gold is a shooting star flying through the sky,
A queen's crown as precious as can be,
A pyramid's hidden treasure,
A field of luscious corn and wheat.

Blue is an ice-cold colour,
A deep azure waterfall,
Waves crashing on the shore,
The River Nile overflowing.

Green is a cat's eye glowing in the dark,
Sour lime spilling from a glass,
A banana's unripe skin,
Holly's prickly leaves.

Lewis Hodgson (9)
Bader Primary School, Thornaby

My Paintbox And Its Colours

Gold is a ray beaming in the sun,
Or a queen's delicate crown,
The sunset in the morning,
Or a shooting star flashing in the night sky.

Red is the petal of a rose,
Or a dragon's flame slashing from his mouth,
A ruby gem twinkling in the twilight,
An apple off a tree.

Black is a cat scratching at a gate,
Or a bird in the night sky,
A sun-filled sky,
Or the rain-filled heavens.

Blue is the summer sky,
Or a bluebird in the wind,
A waterfall falling off the rocks,
Or a sapphire gleaming in the wind.

Green is a calm colour,
Soft, green grass swaying in the wind,
A well-known river sailing through the park,
Or a snake surrounding its prey.

Abbie Pasco (9)
Bader Primary School, Thornaby

As . . .

As free as a bird and as trapped as a prisoner.
As fast as a cheetah and as slow as a snail.
As small as an ant and as big as a whale.
As fierce as a lion and as timid as a mouse.
As short as a bungalow and as tall as a house.
As hot as flames and as cold as frost.
As dark as night and as pale as moonlight.
As black as a witch and as white as a ghost.
As wiggly as a worm and as still as a post.
As yummy as sweets and as yucky as vegetables.
As nasty as to fight and as happy as to share.
As common as the word *the* and as finished as the word *end.*

Aidan Andrews (11)
Bader Primary School, Thornaby

Stars

The stars twinkle and sing so soft,
Up and away in the sky so high.
Little stars you are so bright,
Dancing away into the night.
Oh how you give the gentlest touch,
And how you wink so, so much.
You are shinier than silver foil,
And softer than crumbly soil.
I saw you shoot up in the air,
Through the sky without a care.
You start to sing and I start to cry,
And tears fill up in my eyes.
Oh little star, I love you,
You're the best thing in the whole world.

Becky Cox (9)
Eaterside Primary School, Middlesbrough

Wind

I heard you whistling in the breeze
Over rivers and southern seas
I saw you rustling the tree against my windowpane
And dancing along with the rain.

Sooner than soon you faded away
Until the night
Then you came back with shiver and fright
Twirling and twirling.

Danielle Suggett (9)
Easterside Primary School, Middlesbrough

PS2

On Monday you turned me on and held my hand.
On Tuesday I glared at you with my big square eye.
On Wednesday I ate CDs and caught a virus.
On Thursday I worked on my own at night.
On Friday my top is a brain.
On Saturday my owner bought me some more memory.
On Sunday because I was not plugged in I had a day off.

Matthew Dean (9)
Easterside Primary School, Middlesbrough

My Special Creature

I can hear drumming in my kitchen
And I can hear someone eating food.
I can see big eyes that are looking at me.
It is eating clothes
But you have to feed it
And put in its mouth.
Its legs are small and round.

Micheal Booth (9)
Easterside Primary School, Middlesbrough

Dangerous Dancer

Cheerful checker
Chocolate lover
Super shopper
Dodgy driver
Dangerous dancer
Perfect partier
Terrific teacher
Willing worker.

Jodie Woodier (9)
Easterside Primary School, Middlesbrough

Money Giver

Great swimmer
No smoker
Good climber
Excellent footballer
Crazy fighter
Mad driver
Brilliant sleeper
Money giver.

Robert Woodier (10)
Easterside Primary School, Middlesbrough

My Sisters Are . . .

Sharp shoppers.
Groaner moaners.
Speedy chatterers.
Fashion lovers.
Homework helpers.
Dirty dancers.
Party prancers.
Wild creatures.

Elma Nyauanhu (10)
Easterside Primary School, Middlesbrough

The Wind

Why do you tease,
Steal hats and pinch umbrellas
Then run away in case you get caught,
However, laughing while running?

But I don't understand,
I don't understand.

Why are you so nice,
Cooling us down on a hot summer's day
With your soft breath?
Do you brush your teeth every night?

But I don't understand,
I don't understand.

You tease
But you're so nice.
I love
But I hate you.
I don't understand.

Beth Wilson (10)
Easterside Primary School, Middlesbrough

Flowers

Dancing happily in the summer breeze
Eating up all the bees
Bowing down for a sleep
Then wake up for a peep.

Painted faces
Nodding heads
Brightly coloured
Laid in the flower beds.

Jessica Wilkinson (10)
Easterside Primary School, Middlesbrough

The Moon

I saw you shining up so bright
Up in the sky last night.
I saw you going in the morning
But when you are gone it is so boring.
I know you sing in glee
You are friendly to everyone even a bee.
I saw you shining up so bright
Up in the sky last night.

I saw you lonely as a little flower
If you go I'll be sad.
If you go I'll be sad
Please don't go, if you do I will send you a letter.
If you come back I'll be better.
Yes, you've come back to me
But if you want I'll let you go
And let you go and let you be.
I saw you shining up so bright
Up in the sky last night.

Danielle Raby (9)
Easterside Primary School, Middlesbrough

Snowy Poem!

I see you kissing the windowpane,
I see you dancing with the rain.
I hear you tiptoeing on the roof,
And my dog gives a big woof!
You somersault down from the sky,
While the birds are flying high.

You dance and flip and whirl with glee,
You float down on the Queen's Jubilee.
You fall and fall all through Christmas time,
And then at summertime,
You melt, melt and melt and . . . gone.

Sarah Louise Bedford (9)
Easterside Primary School, Middlesbrough

Clash Of Lightning

I stared up at the
Dark sky to watch
Your light show or
Was it just my eyes,
We rarely see you on the street,
But we know why.

Oh lightning, oh lightning,
Oh lightning in the dark sky.

You glare down at us
As we say why, oh why?
I've seen you slice through trees,
Not a nice sight!

Oh lightning, oh lightning,
Oh lightning in the dark sky.

But why, oh why?

Oh lightning in the dark sky.

Bradley Pluves (10)
Easterside Primary School, Middlesbrough

The Snow

I saw you way up high,
Somersaulting from the sky.
I noticed you kiss the top of the tree,
I even saw you wave at me.
The breeze blew you away,
And it took you a day.

Oh snow, oh snow, I see you going,
Oh snow, oh snow, please don't go!
I don't know what I'll do without you,
I spy on you from way up high,
And you made the sky look so wide.

Lauren Stevenson (10)
Easterside Primary School, Middlesbrough

The Tornado

I saw you demolishing all the land,
And then you twist up all the trees,
You look around to terrorise something else,
You look so scary from down below,
You're so loud,
You're so scary, please go away.

When I saw you look so strange,
You twist at horrendous speed,
You are deadly and are horrifying,
Your screams are very loud, you are too loud,
You're so loud,
You're so scary, please go away.

Now the land is all torn up,
Please go away, go away,
You're so scary, go away,
You are so horrifying,
You're so loud,
You're so scary, go away.

Gabrielle Blanchard (10)
Easterside Primary School, Middlesbrough

Rainbow

You set a smile across the sky
You brighten up the day.
I see a bright light
And I know you're coming this way.
You have lots of money as people always say
And someone will find it one eventual day.
You're also rich in colour
You are bright
And I bet if you stayed
You would shine in the night.
But then you have to go
And we can't find treasure anymore.

Jessica Cromack (9)
Easterside Primary School, Middlesbrough

The Waterfall

I saw you poking animals,
And I saw you diving down into the water,
I heard you shout,
Trying to say, 'Get out!'
I see you hammering the water,
And I see you swimming with the fish.

I saw all the things you did,
But always you hid,
You twinkle like a piece of gold,
Even though you are so bold,
I see you covering the fish,
And I see you smiling
As you go in the sun.

Lewis McGarrity (9)
Easterside Primary School, Middlesbrough

The Snow

I saw you somersault from the sky,
I even saw you way up high.
I noticed you kissing the top of the trees,
As they swayed in the breeze.
Oh snow, oh snow, I saw you coming,
Oh snow, oh snow, I saw you going.
I watched you drive the bees away,
On a cold, winter day.
I saw you playing in the park,
I saw you making my dog bark.
Oh snow, oh snow, I saw you coming,
Oh snow, oh snow, I saw you go.

Louisa Watson (9)
Easterside Primary School, Middlesbrough

Wind!

I see you play
With the clouds,
You play tig
And run around,
You toss and turn
On your back,
I see you jump
And make a draught,
At summertime you
Seem so gentle,
You swish and you
Turn with the bees,
I hear you singing
All day long.
You sing so loud
The birds join in,
At autumn time you
Throw the leaves
And bump into trees,
You bounce off windows,
Bounce of floors,
You turn around and
Bounce off walls.
Now it's time to say
Goodbye, let's see you
Another time.

Tanya Herlingshaw (10)
Easterside Primary School, Middlesbrough

Tick-Tock

Tick-tock goes my heart
My food is like AA batteries
I sing a song that goes ding-dong
When my two hands turn twelve
At night my eyes light up.

Kevin Horsfield (9)
Easterside Primary School, Middlesbrough

The Snow

I saw you
throw the white
light snow at
my brand new
window as I
saw you pass
while covering my grass. I
see you wrapping
your cold
arms around me
while you fold
your legs.

I see you
covering the
people round
the countryside
while they
slide down.

Jake Bringloe (9)
Easterside Primary School, Middlesbrough

Snow-White Snow

I saw you somersault from the sky
As you kissed our rooftops high.

You roly-poly across our lawn
Tomorrow, tomorrow out in the dawn.

Spinning down from the clouds
Landing in the carol crowds.

Snowmen all over
Bring back the clover.

Thomas Gainford (10)
Easterside Primary School, Middlesbrough

The Snow

I saw you kiss the silent countryside,
I saw you cap the top of icy mountains.

I heard you sing the sweetest song,
I heard you as the wind hurried you along.

I thought about you wiping out all the bees,
I thought about you giving all of the humans a shivery breeze.

I touched you like an icy shock,
I touched you like a chilly monster that scared all of the flock.

I smelt you with the crisp of the dew,
I smelt you like you were very new.

Now Christmas is fading so I can't see the snow,
Hear the snow, think about the snow,
Touch the snow or smell the snow.

Adam Bland (10)
Easterside Primary School, Middlesbrough

Snow!

I saw you kiss the top of my hat
And you came down as fast as a cat.

I saw you roly poly in the sky
And dance on the rooftops high.

As you ran across our lawn
You coloured in the sky to dawn.

As you rolled up in a tight ball
As you flung yourself into a wall.

Ryan Marley (10)
Easterside Primary School, Middlesbrough

Tornado

I saw you rip up all the ground,
All the things that I'd found,
You ate up all the food I'd got
To you I am a tiny dot.

Oh twister, twisting all day long,
Oh twister, whistling the loudest song.

I saw you demolish a football stadium,
I even saw you at the Palladium.

Oh twister, twisting all day long,
Oh twister, whistling the loudest song.

Straight away your speed will beat me,
You will get a gold medal very, very easily.

Robert Bland (10)
Easterside Primary School, Middlesbrough

The Snow

I saw you playing in the breeze
You were doing whatever you pleased.
As you kissed the top of my tree
I walked by and you dropped on me.
It was cold but never mind
Because we played down the valley,
We played down the park,
We even played in my own backyard,
We played down the beach,
I even bought a peach
But now the summer's back,
You melted away.

Amy Laverick (9)
Easterside Primary School, Middlesbrough

The Clouds

I saw you stroll across the sky
Like a snail on a hot day.
Why do you hide behind the sun
And block the light to the world?
O clouds, moving across the sky,
O clouds, way up high.

When you change your clothes from white to black
And cry sad songs I always feel unhappy,
Until you change back
And I feel happy again.
O clouds, moving in the sky,
O clouds, way up high.

Emily Gibson (10)
Easterside Primary School, Middlesbrough

Snow On Snow

When you chased off all the bees
I saw you tumble and kiss the trees
You're the lightest snow I've ever seen
Soft like velvet, ever clean, you're just the dream
You always get pushed
The children always say, 'Hush!'
As you fall off the roofs
Everyone dances to the moves
Snow, snow, fall at night
Snow, snow, all so bright.

Ben Snaith (10)
Easterside Primary School, Middlesbrough

The Wind!

You, the cold wind,
You gave me a chill,
You're sitting there blowing
And nodding like Churchill.
You gave me the flu.
It makes me sneeze,
Atishoo! Atishoo!

Rebecca Bastiman (10)
Easterside Primary School, Middlesbrough

Conker Cracker

Park finder
Hard hitter
Conker cracker
Free faller
Shell breaker
Field finder
Vinegar soaker.

John Hagan (9)
Easterside Primary School, Middlesbrough

Wild Hugger

Good cleaner
Hard sleeper
TV watcher
Never nagger
Homework helper
Computer player
Wild hugger.

Jon Iseton (9)
Easterside Primary School, Middlesbrough

Chin Crusher

Chin crusher
Sweaty trainer
Shadow boxer
Up cutter
Mirror lookers
Ring fighter
Speed puncher
Skipper winner.

Kenneth Woodier (10)
Easterside Primary School, Middlesbrough

Boxing Dancer

Speed puncher
Nose cruncher
Boxing dancer
Body builder
Ear basher
Eye crusher
Chin chinned
Glory winner.

Scott Jones (10)
Easterside Primary School, Middlesbrough

Super Sisters Are . . .

Groaner moaners
Champion chatterers
Disco divas
Daft dancers
Fashion lovers
Hate brothers.

Alexandra Brady (10)
Easterside Primary School, Middlesbrough

Can You Guess?

Saddle carrier
Polo muncher
Stable liver
Tail swisher
Noise maker
Speed waver
Grass eater
Hard worker.

Jessica Smith (10)
Easterside Primary School, Middlesbrough

Cats

Four hander
Fast runner
Card cutter
String player
Finger licker
Nose twitcher
Basket scratcher.

Laura McMenamin (10)
Easterside Primary School, Middlesbrough

PlayStation 2

I eat CDs and spit them out.
I have a virus.
I glare at you with my screen.
I have a magnificent memory.
I talk and sing and shout and scream.
I have a brilliant brain with a green light.
I work on my own at night.

Andrew Berry (9)
Easterside Primary School, Middlesbrough

The Underground Train

In the dark, dark night there is a squiggly worm train under
the ground

Its eyes are like lights
Its wheels go fast like legs running in a race
Its buttons are working like my brain
When it engine warms up it beats like my heart
The chairs inside it are like a tummy
Soft and cuddly.

Thomas Arnold (9)
Easterside Primary School, Middlesbrough

The Shoe

I have laces for hair
I talk when I walk
I have a pointed nose
I have four eyes
I have a big, long mouth with a black tongue
I have lots of marks from scraping the floor
I bet you have a few.
I am, of course, a shoe!

Megan Williams (9)
Easterside Primary School, Middlesbrough

Team Winner

Super striker
Dirty tackler
Speedy runner
Team winner
Goal saver
Brillo marker
Perfect passer
Pro player.

Jamie Lee Wells (9)
Easterside Primary School, Middlesbrough

Autumn Is Coming

It's autumn
And the garden is changing its clothes
Putting away
Its bright green skirts
Its dazzling shorts
And blazing yellow dresses.

Now it cocoons itself in dark brown wellington boots
Slips on dull grey coats
Sleeved with amber and black scarves
Pulls on woolly hats of conkers and leaves
Violet socks and dark blue trainers
Then relaxes in the bright moonlight.

Sam Gunn (9)
Hutton Rudby Primary School, Hutton Rudby

Autumn

It's autumn
And the garden is changing its clothes
Putting away
Its dazzling sunflower hats
Its scarlet-rose tops
And sky-blue skirts.

Now it wraps itself in dusty, brown scarves
Slips on woolly, dark jumpers
And mucky, brown trousers
Pulls on its dim, green wellies
And conker shell hats
Then hides in the gloomy shadows.

Sarah McAsey (9)
Hutton Rudby Primary School, Hutton Rudby

Autumn Is Here

Autumn is here
And my leaves are turning gold and bronze
And are cascading to the ground
As I look down
I see the primrose flowers that surround me are dead
I look around the garden
Everything is dying
A blanket of leaves is spread across the floor
The sun has gone down
Autumn is here.

Autumn is here
Spring has gone
The grass has disappeared
And the clouds are coming
A picnic rug of frost has landed over my leaves
The pink roses that surround the garden turn brown
And will bud next year
Autumn is here.

Becky Devereux (9)
Hutton Rudby Primary School, Hutton Rudby

Autumn Has Come

Autumn has come
And the garden is changing its clothes,
Putting away
Sunhats, suncream, shorts and T-shirts.
Shedding off its red, yellow, orange and brown dress
As the crusty leaves cascade to the ground.

Now it gets out its conker trousers,
Leafy, long-sleeved tops, pompom hats,
Woolly scarves and gloves and muddy wellies.
Summer has gone.

Rachael Boyle (9)
Hutton Rudby Primary School, Hutton Rudby

The Nightmare Spell

Round about the bed I go,
In the bed you I throw.
Then I chuck in some bats,
Some spiders, worms and nasty cats.
Now I'm going to let you rot,
And I'll make you dinner in the cauldron pot.

Poach and scramble, bake and fry.
If you scream I'll make you die.
Hubble, bubble, chop and heat.
You had better be ready to eat.

Rather than taking milk to bed,
Take some eyeballs and goo instead.
In the cauldron, boil and bubble.
Here's a spell that will cause trouble.
Now the broth is ready to eat.
This will be a nasty treat.

Poach and scramble, bake and fry.
If you scream I'll make you die.
Hubble, bubble, chop and heat.
You had better be ready to eat.

Mark Artley (9)
Hutton Rudby Primary School, Hutton Rudby

Autumn Is Here

Autumn is here
And the tree is putting away its acid-green jumpers,
Leaves are cascading then turning chocolate-brown,
The garden is putting away its rainbow overcoats
And bringing the frosty skirts out for another year.

Autumn is here.

Sebastian Langston (9)
Hutton Rudby Primary School, Hutton Rudby

Around The World

Round about the cauldron go
In the Great Pyramid of Giza we throw
Add a plane
And travel to Spain
As Spain is the place to be
As you travel over land and sea.

Boil and pop, boil and pop
Place the world in the cooking pot.

In the cauldron grill the Great Wall of China
And come to this lovely diner
Travel all over
And end up in Dover.

Boil and pop, boil and pop
Place the world in the cooking pot.

Jacob Straw (10)
Hutton Rudby Primary School, Hutton Rudby

Chocolate

Galaxy, Mars bar, Milky Way too
Here's a treat for me and you
Chocolate drops are for cakes
Though I just eat them with chocolate snakes
Chocolate goes with a midnight feast
I know I have to eat my veg
But I'll tip it in the hedge
So don't give me veg, give me *chocolate!*

Harriet Atkinson (9)
Hutton Rudby Primary School, Hutton Rudby

How To Make A Terrifying Werewolf

Round about the wooden cauldron goes
In goes a bold wolf we throw
Now a pinch of horses' manes goes
In we throw some full moon stones
Next we add a slimy newt's tail
In we put a kid who is male.

Whisk and cut, whisk and cut
Add a filthy mutt
Bake and steam, bake and steam
Here's a spell to make you scream!

Blend it in with a forest dead
Mix in with a skeleton's head
Now put a big balloon
And a piece of full moon
And fry some evil eyes
Now stew some dangerous lies.

Whisk and cut, whisk and cut
Add a filthy mutt
Bake and steam, bake and steam
Here's a spell to make you scream!

Harry Kitching (9)
Hutton Rudby Primary School, Hutton Rudby

What A Dragon Will Eat

What a dragon will eat
Is a mountain of meat.
He'll eat cows, sheep and dogs
He will even eat huge hogs!
He'll fry, cook and bake
And wash it down with a great big lake!

Jack Martin Williamson (9)
Hutton Rudby Primary School, Hutton Rudby

A Spell To Make A Best Friend

Round about the pond we go
In the rosy cheeks we throw
Spread the smile across the face
Drop in strawberry lace
Sprinkle in the fragment petal
Pour in the joy from a kettle.

Stir and simmer, stir and simmer
This will really make you shimmer
Poach and brew, poach and brew
You will really feel brand new.

Place in the lovely sharing
And throw in all the caring
Your friendship will never end
Drink this potion then get a friend
Do not put in any hate
Then this will make you a perfect mate.

Stir and simmer, stir and simmer
This will really make you shimmer
Poach and brew, poach and brew
You will really feel brand new.

Sophie Victoria Robinson (9)
Hutton Rudby Primary School, Hutton Rudby

Autumn Is Here

It's autumn,
And the garden is changing its clothes,
Putting away its rose-red skirts,
Its golden flower sun hats,
And its blouses of violets and sunflowers.

Then it pulls on its dark brown overcoats,
Its drab, brown tracksuits,
And the trees undress, getting ready to go to sleep in winter,
Autumn is here.

Aidan Broadhurst (9)
Hutton Rudby Primary School, Hutton Rudby

A Spell To Wake The Dead

Add some bones from their grave,
Put it in the pot to bathe.
Go down to Hell to get their souls,
And in the pot we add some moles.
Put in a swamp lizard's tongue,
Mix it with some spiders' dung.

Slice and steam, slice and steam,
Listen to the people scream.
Chop and grind, chop and grind,
In this pot we'll make mankind.

Add a snake's fang or two,
Whisk it up until it's goo.
Into the pot we'll add a rat,
Cover with a lice-infested hat.
Put in a jar of gruesome moths,
Heat it up until it froths.

Slice and steam, slice and steam,
Listen to the people scream.
Chop and grind, chop and grind,
In this pot we'll make mankind.

William Loader (10)
Hutton Rudby Primary School, Hutton Rudby

Birthday

I am excited about my birthday
Like a flower is eager for the sun
Like a dog is excited about a bone
Like a bird is thrilled by spring
Like a key is eager to open
Like a football is ecstatic about a foot
I am excited about my birthday.

Matthew Hodgson (9)
Hutton Rudby Primary School, Hutton Rudby

Autumn Is Here

Autumn is coming,
The garden is pulling off its dazzling sunshine tops
And its emerald-green leaf sandals
Then its primrose sun hats and closing them into a cupboard.

Next the garden opens a different cupboard
And puts on its chocolate chestnut jumper
And bronze conker trousers
Also it puts on its blushing grass-green, shiny apple, woolly hat
And its wellies of amber and tanned leaves
Then it warms up by the blaze of the bonfire.

Christopher Loader (10)
Hutton Rudby Primary School, Hutton Rudby

Autumn Time

It's autumn and fresh water is starting to fall from the sky
The tree is taking off its brown, leafy jumper
The haily wind is blowing harder and harder
Branches blowing everywhere
The garden pulls on its red, brown and orange jumper and says,
'Off, you sunflower shorts!'

Alexander Rogers (9)
Hutton Rudby Primary School, Hutton Rudby

It's Autumn

Crispy, golden and crimson leaves, cascading down
On the silver, sparkling grass
Torn up petals of scarlet and white littering the garden
Hedgehogs scurrying through the frosted bushes, gathering food
And leaves for winter.

Philip Hutchinson (9)
Hutton Rudby Primary School, Hutton Rudby

A Spell To Make You Lucky

Round about the cauldron we go
In the charms we have to throw
Now for the lucky padlock
Don't forget the green shamrock
Put in the leprechaun gold
But make sure there is no mould.

Sizzle and brew, sizzle and brew
Now for the horseshoe.

Now please take a seat
As we add the rabbit feet
It's time for the four-leaved clover
Now that it is nearly over
Time for the lottery ticket
It's nearly time for them to pick it.

Sizzle and brew, sizzle and brew
Now for the horseshoe.

Elena Leyshon (9)
Hutton Rudby Primary School, Hutton Rudby

Autumn Is Here

The crisp, crimson leaves cascade silently to the ground
As the tree prepares for the long slumber ahead
Animals harvest food to fill up their stores
The fire jumps about fighting as it eats up logs
The spider's silk is freshly polished with dewdrops
The flowers start withering as the days grow darker
As it grows colder the frost comes like an icy river
The sun goes down.

Autumn is here.

Craig Lockyer (10)
Hutton Rudby Primary School, Hutton Rudby

A Spell To Make Your Eyes Pop Out!

Round about the cauldron we go,
In the cooking pot we will throw:
Maggot-coated haggis and stew,
A human eyeball, leave to brew,
Grill the bogies and slice in Hell,
Quick, quick, quick, let's finish the spell.

Hubble, bubble, toilet trouble,
Mix it up right at the double.

Take a cigar, toast it well,
Poach the flies and spread the spell,
Toilet juice and elephant dung,
Warning: this will kill the lung,
Add the lumpy bits of sick,
Now stir it up with a poisoned stick.

Hubble, bubble, toilet trouble,
Mix it up right at the double.

Bethany Brown (9)
Hutton Rudby Primary School, Hutton Rudby

It's Autumn

It's autumn,
And the garden is changing its clothes,
Putting away its radiant leaf T-shirts,
Bird nest sun hats,
And shorts of moist bark.

Now it wraps itself in a grass shirt,
Pulls on a fluffy cloud coat,
And crusty frost trousers.

As the year slowly creeps on,
It sleeps peacefully in the moonlight.
Autumn is here.

Bruce Hall (9)
Hutton Rudby Primary School, Hutton Rudby

A Spell To Make You Scream!

Round about the cauldron go
In a bag of trembles throw
Quickly add a pint of tears
Blend it with a bottle of fears
Next you need some werewolf hair
Then sprinkle in some scary nightmare.

Whisk and bake, whisk and bake
Cut a slice of gruesome cake
Offer round, offer round
Watch ghosts fall on the ground.

Brew it with a drop of blood
Next pour in a sweaty flood
Scramble in an evil stare
This is not a spell to share
Simmer with a devil's laughter
Then barbecue the whole thing after.

Whisk and bake, whisk and bake
Cut a slice of gruesome cake
Offer round, offer round
Watch ghosts fall on the ground.

Georgia E J Slade (9)
Hutton Rudby Primary School, Hutton Rudby

Trains

A good transport they are,
They can take you a long way by far.
They run on steam and coal,
Faster than a young foal.
Coated with nice paint,
To get on it you just can't wait!

Benjamin Russell Butterworth (9)
Hutton Rudby Primary School, Hutton Rudby

Autumn Is Coming

It's autumn and the leaves are changing colour
To red, yellow, orange and brown
Then the crisp leaves are cascading from the trees
Hedgehogs hibernate ready for the winter months
New fantastic fruits are ripening brambles, apples, pears
And lots more
Animals are filling their cupboards ready for the winter months
Children are collecting conkers
Ready for conker fights with their friends
People are making apple pie and apple crumble
A burning fire will be lit in the dark, autumn nights
As the sun falls down more and more shadows are appearing
Autumn is here.

Harry Dodds (9)
Hutton Rudby Primary School, Hutton Rudby

Autumn's Return

The garden is taking off its silky, summer dresses
and short sleeves and storing them away in the cupboard,
She is changing them for brown, leafy jumpers
with conker buttons and emerald-blue, watery trousers,
The grass has turned into a solid silver carpet
with dewdrops shimmering like diamonds,
A silky conker shell lies open next to its glistening cargo,
A spider's web shimmering
as if God Himself has polished it with an angel's cloak,
The sun breaks through the clouds
covering the floor with a misty light,
Autumn has returned.

Callum Curtis (9)
Hutton Rudby Primary School, Hutton Rudby

A Spell For A Perfect World

First put in a punnet of peace
So war will boil away and cease.
Pour in a drop of solution
To put an end to all pollution.

Stir and slice, stir and slice
This will make the whole world nice.

Add a large slice of health
And a good sprinkle of wealth.
Mix in a gallon of rain
And a tiny squeeze of pain.

Stir and slice, stir and slice
This will make the whole world nice.

Rachael Cook (9)
Hutton Rudby Primary School, Hutton Rudby

My Cat Is A Crazy Cat

My cat is a crazy cat
He's always chasing a fly
He chases and chases
And chases until the fly
Jumps into the sky!

Andrew Hughes (9)
Hutton Rudby Primary School, Hutton Rudby

When The Ghosts Come

I turn my head to see a bare tree
Where a crow squawking its ghostly laugh sits.
The dark clouds cover the sky like black cotton balls.
Statues stare dimly at passers-by.
The gates close.
The ghosts come out.

Jordan Andrew Wright (10)
Linthorpe Community Primary School, Middlesbrough

Autumn

Shiny, smooth conkers,
Children knocking them down
With long, thickened sticks.
Squirrels scurrying all
Around and climbing
Trees to gather nuts
And acorns.

Birds humming in the
Nests singing like a
Baby wailing.
Crows swooping down
Like a crashing wave.
Berries, ruby-red, like
Blood and as sour as
Lemons.

Naila Arif (10)
Linthorpe Community Primary School, Middlesbrough

Night-Time

Owls hooting
Car doors slamming
Music playing
Wind swaying

Books falling
People talking
Pencils falling
TV playing.

Bedtime
Night-time
Sleep time.

Liam French (7)
Linthorpe Community Primary School, Middlesbrough

The Cemetery

The crispy leaves
Falling off the crooked trees
Golden-brown conkers
Smooth, shiny and round
The wind rushing like
The tide crashing against
The rocks
Crows squawking past trees
Gathering together on beheaded
Gravestones
The smells from the sweet
And sour berries
The grass swaying in
The breeze
The smell of flowers
Sweet as a freshly-
Picked bunch of lilies.

Mahak Riaz (10)
Linthorpe Community Primary School, Middlesbrough

The Night

In the night shadows behind your curtains
Car doors slamming next door
Cats purring, bats flapping
I feel scared
Moon shining
Lightning flashing and clashing
Ankle grabbers on the stairs
Police walking in the street
It's a scary night!

Zoe Widdowfield (7)
Linthorpe Community Primary School, Middlesbrough

The Forest

In the trees there are bees
On the ground minibeasts are found
In a box lives a fox
In a hole lives a mole
In the air birds are there
Near a lair lives a bear
On the ground lives a hound
On the leaves minibeasts are thieves
In the night vipers fight
In the brambles there are shambles
On the branch there are bats with funny hats
People fear the horns of a deer.

Oliver Simpson (10)
Linthorpe Community Primary School, Middlesbrough

Nature's Calling

Through the swaying trees I see ponds
Rippling in the wailing winds,
I touch the soggy mud oozing onto my wellies,
I see minibeasts crawling on the ground making the leaves rustle,
I hear birds cooing high in the trees making their nests,
I taste the brambles from the bushes in my mouth,
I smell the air so different to what I smell back at home!

Catherine Regan (9)
Linthorpe Community Primary School, Middlesbrough

Night-Time

Water dripping, lightning flashing, cats on the prowl, *howl!*
Doors banging, floorboards creaking, spooky visions, *scared!*
Ghosts and monsters, scary shadows, creepy voices, *freaky!*
Ghostly thunder, knives clattering, creepy hands, *worried!*
Owls screeching, bats flapping, dogs barking, *creepy!*

Amy Keegan (7)
Linthorpe Community Primary School, Middlesbrough

Night-Time

Car doors slamming,
Light downstairs,
Bears roaring, brothers snoring,
Night-time, night-time, light and dark time,
Garden gates closing,
Water dripping,
Dogs barking,
Hands and voices are being used,
Light time and dark time,
Light is day
And dark is night.

Benjamin Honeysett (7)
Linthorpe Community Primary School, Middlesbrough

Conkers

Conkers
The smooth side slides out of the shell.
They start to go crisp and brown.
The shell cuddles the shiny conker with its protective spikes.
Children choose their conkers wisely
as they battle in the old tree house.

Lewis Southall (10)
Linthorpe Community Primary School, Middlesbrough

Night-Time

Feeling scared and lonely
Faces in the curtains
Clocks ticking
Ghosts hiding, monsters creeping,
Ankle grabbers
Nightmares in my head.

Freya Heselton (8)
Linthorpe Community Primary School, Middlesbrough

What Am I?

My furry coat is brown and red,
I have pointy ears upon my head,
I only come out at night,
I give people an awful fright,
I have a very bushy tail,
I catch my prey without fail,
I have four paws and run very fast.
Catching my prey, I'm never last.
What am I?

Emma Pallister (9)
Linthorpe Community Primary School, Middlesbrough

In The Night

Ankle grabbers on the stairs
And monsters in my curtains.
Moon shining, stars twinkling
People talking, dogs barking.
People laughing, people crying
And now it's sleep time.

Owen Waddington (7)
Linthorpe Community Primary School, Middlesbrough

Night-Time

Seeing light above my head.
Hearing dogs - woof woof!
People snoring.
Owls creeping and squirrels sleeping.
Shadows dancing in the curtains.
I like night-time.

Jack Farrow (7)
Linthorpe Community Primary School, Middlesbrough

What Am I?

I have great colours of brown and red,
I only come out at night.
I have a short but bushy tail,
I stalk through the forest looking for food.
I can take over a rabbit's burrow,
I improve it and make it my own.
I am very rare, I am being hunted down,
I have four paws and run very fast.
What am I?

Katy Farrow (10)
Linthorpe Community Primary School, Middlesbrough

In The Night

People talking in the hall
Monsters knocking on the door
Freaky things in the bed
Cats running on the floor
Dogs howling in the hall
Owls hooting in the trees
Floorboards creaking in the hall
Car doors slamming
People coming home late.

Abbi English (7)
Linthorpe Community Primary School, Middlesbrough

Who Am I?

My coat is ginger and bright,
My eyes sparkle in the night.
I leave my lair to catch my prey,
Watch out! I'm coming *there*.
So next time you might see me if I dare!

Alex Cane (9)
Linthorpe Community Primary School, Middlesbrough

Who Am I?

I am tall,
As the creamy blue sky.
I grow up,
So, so high.
I am dark brown,
And grassy green.
You can see me,
For a mile or two.
I live in a beautiful country,
And gloomy forests.
I start as a seed,
Birds flutter near me.
I have long arms,
But no legs.
I am an organism,
Kids climb me.
I hold leaves,
I am a . . .?

Laura Cooper (9)
Linthorpe Community Primary School, Middlesbrough

The Cemetery

One autumn day
Lazy snails
Sleeping on the cool
Stones
Leaving
Swirling, silver trails
Behind them on
The gravestones
Decorating
The letters
With glittery
Lines . . .

Harun Hussain (10)
Linthorpe Community Primary School, Middlesbrough

Cemetery

Leaves turning gold
And crisp.
Shiny, brown conkers
Cracked open.
Squirrels scampering
And scuttling through
The golden leaves to
Find them.

The breeze hitting
The autumn trees
Softly so they
Sway.
An unusual leaf
Covered in brown and
Black spots
Just like a
Leopard covered in spots.
The scent of damp
Rotten leaves fills
The air but still
Some dandelions fighting
Through the ground.

Nawal Forbes (10)
Linthorpe Community Primary School, Middlesbrough

Cold

Cold is blue like the sky
It sounds like a clock ticking
It feels like ice
It looks like snow
It smells like two strong mints
It tastes like sour apples.

Joseph Huck (9)
Linthorpe Community Primary School, Middlesbrough

Pinchinthorpe - A Sense Poem

In Pinchinthorpe forest you can see
all the different kinds of trees.

In Pinchinthorpe forest you can hear
all the different birds in the trees.

In Pinchinthorpe forest you can feel
the air as it tickles up your spine.

In Pinchinthorpe forest you can taste
all the brambles on the bushes.

In Pinchinthorpe forest you can smell
all the different kinds of flowers.

Pinchinthorpe forest is a fun place to be.

Jack Hart (10)
Linthorpe Community Primary School, Middlesbrough

Forest On The Move

I can hear birds cooing high in the pine trees,
I can feel the whirling wind against me,
I can see rain falling and rippling the ponds,
I can taste the brambles rattling on the bushes.

I can see the wood on the floor,
I can feel the soggy mud under my feet,
I can see little insects below me,
I can hear squirrels collecting nuts in the woods.

I can taste the country air,
I can smell the coloured flowers all around,
I can hear the splashes of fish in the pond,
All is on the move in the forest.

Jessica Rogers (9)
Linthorpe Community Primary School, Middlesbrough

Autumn

In autumn,
Squirrels start springing,
Nibbling conkers that are as shiny
As a silver coin,
Off beautiful horse chestnut trees.

In autumn,
Prickly pine leaves, like a hedgehog
Whirled up in a ball,
Are scattered on the cold, hard ground.

In autumn,
Birds and animals,
Prepare for winter,
Making habitats into a home,
So they can drift off to sleep.

Elizabeth Hewitson (11)
Linthorpe Community Primary School, Middlesbrough

Autumn Is Beginning

Moss growing in cracks and grooves
Soft, green and damp
Squirrels scurrying, collecting acorns
Looking around mischievously
Six o'clock, getting cold and dark
Owls perched on branches
Conkers falling
Tumbling down like a misplaced bowling ball
Birds flying overhead calling as they go
Leaves dancing in the breeze
Like puppets being operated by strings
Steamy car windows, cold and foggy.
This is how autumn begins.

Sam Fletcher (10)
Linthorpe Community Primary School, Middlesbrough

The Cemetery

Birds singing happily
Flying through the bright sky.
Silent squirrels scatter through golden, crispy leaves.
The air is fresh,
Trees swaying side to side,
Their long arms trying to hug you.
Conker cases prickly like a hedgehog
But soft inside like a velvet cloak.
Quiet gravestones, grey
But decorated with colourful, bright flowers.

Charlotte Reney (10)
Linthorpe Community Primary School, Middlesbrough

The Great Oak Tree

The great oak tree stands tall,
As high as the moon itself.

The great oak tree's old, bumpy bark,
Is like a cobbled pathway never-ending.

The great oak tree's leaves rustle in the wind,
Louder than a million football fans screaming.

The great tree is a very graceful, living thing.

Andrew Horkan (10)
Linthorpe Community Primary School, Middlesbrough

What Am I?

My coat is black and white
I catch my prey at night
My eyes sparkle brightly
I am scared of humans.
What am I?

Nicole Rodgers (9)
Linthorpe Community Primary School, Middlesbrough

The Lonely Little Evergreen

In autumn time
The first leaf falls
But
None from the little evergreen
That stays green all year round
In winter
When wet winds blow
No rustling now
Not like in autumn
All that is only the little evergreen
That it is green then
When spring comes all the leaves return
The little evergreen
Remembers long, winter visits
And hopes he won't come back.

Iona Loughran (10)
Linthorpe Community Primary School, Middlesbrough

The Autumn Tree

In the cemetery
When autumn is here
Branches start to rustle
Leaves drift and float
Onto the bright green grass.

The autumn tree
Has huge, brown, thick, bumpy branches
Like arms to hold the crispy red and yellow leaves.

Bark like unbreakable, thick metal
Dropped on the ground.
Roots are creamy, rich and brown
With a long, lumpy shape
Thick as a bone wall.

Nadine Al-Asadi (10)
Linthorpe Community Primary School, Middlesbrough

A Poem For A Roman Soldier

Here's my Roman soldier,
He stands so very tall.
When he looks down at his enemies,
They look very small.
My soldier is very strong
And really likes to fight,
He fights in the day
And in the night.
His top is made of armour;
His shield is made of wood,
The Romans weren't just nasty,
They were also very good.

Kate Conyard (8)
Linthorpe Community Primary School, Middlesbrough

The Cemetery

Birds tweeting
Squirrels running
All you can smell is fresh air
People walking
Grass is swaying
Squirrels leaping while graves are silent
Conkers falling
While a quiet wind blows
Insects crawling
Trees are rotting
Underfoot is smooth and soft.

Eve O'Malley (10)
Linthorpe Community Primary School, Middlesbrough

A Squirrel's Tale

Scuttling along the tree I go
Waving my tail in the air
Collecting conkers as I go
Waving my tail in the air
Some may see me but never will catch me
Waving my tail in the air.

With my beady, black eyes I may look cute
Waving my tail in the air
But fear me you may for my small, sharp teeth
Waving my tail in the air
For I am not tame, like a dog or a cat
Waving my tail in the air.

Conkers I eat, for they are good
Waving my tail in the air
Now back to my warm, cosy drey I must go
Waving my tail in the air
As I go
Waving my tail in the air.

Charis Featherstone (10)
Linthorpe Community Primary School, Middlesbrough

Cemetery In Autumn

Autumn leaves pounding on the ground
Make me believe it's as fantastic as you tell me.
Sticks on the ground going *snap!*
Crispy leaves on the ground.
Conkers running away from the wind.
Wet and windy weather - make it stop!
Birds singing up high in the trees.

Gemma Braithwaite (10)
Linthorpe Community Primary School, Middlesbrough

Midnight At The Cemetery

Midnight at the cemetery
When nobody is there,
Leaves start to rustle like a baby's rattle,
Trees begin to move around.

Midnight at the cemetery
Gravestones shake and shiver,
Ghosts appear everywhere
Hovering above the ground.

Midnight at the cemetery
Owls start to shout,
Wolves begin to howl
With an echoing sound.

Emily Wheatley (10)
Linthorpe Community Primary School, Middlesbrough

Autumn Animals

Birds shoot through the trees,
High sky,
Like an aeroplane going
Full speed.

Squirrels run as fast as lightning,
On the murky pathway,
Like a bullet cutting through
Fresh air.

Owls swoop down at night
To catch their prey,
Like a hunter chasing
A fox.

Jack Burns (10)
Linthorpe Community Primary School, Middlesbrough

Autumn

In autumn,
When leaves fall off trees,
Squirrels leap
As high as hares, brown and white.

In autumn,
When leaves fall off trees,
Birds sing and hum
While grey and white squirrels collect
Bold, brown conkers for freezing winter.

In autumn,
When leaves fall off trees,
The seven seas
Are as dark and grey as muddy puddles.

Zeeshan Mehmood (10)
Linthorpe Community Primary School, Middlesbrough

Cemetery Scares

Creepy at night, you'd better beware,
If you don't you'll get a scare!
Creepy at night, you'll need to stay safe,
You'd better keep away from the dead people's grave.
Not scary anymore, now it's the day,
Everyone's happy, you might as well stay,
Not scary anymore, birds singing sweetly,
And now you can see that you are free,
The cemetery may look really scary at night,
But in the day you won't get a fright,
It may look as sweet as chocolate now,
But just you wait till the sun goes down!

Hayley Harrowsmith (10)
Linthorpe Community Primary School, Middlesbrough

The Cemetery In Autumn

Under my feet rustling leaves,
Overhead a squirrel scurrying away.
All over my body cold shivers.
Trees swaying side to side, their long branches like arms dancing.

Twigs snapping under my feet,
I can see how many memories have faded away,
It makes me sad, I think I may cry.

Shiny, brown conkers scattered on the muddy ground,
Some broken, rotten, mouldy.
Others glow, shine.
Echoes of a group of children, half poor, half rich.

Nyla Akhtar (10)
Linthorpe Community Primary School, Middlesbrough

Autumn

In autumn,
When leaves fall
Off trees,
Squirrels leap as high as hares,
Autumn winds blow swiftly,
Picking up leaves as they go,
Conkers in a warm blanket,
Fall off ancient horse chestnut trees,
Birds sing beautifully in their nests,
Squirrels collect millions of nuts,
Stocking up for cold winter,
Snails lay silver tracks in the golden sun.

Michael Edon (10)
Linthorpe Community Primary School, Middlesbrough

The Romantic Sun

The sun is hot as lava
The sun is as red as your lips
The sun is bright and happy
So you can do swimming and quick dips.

The sun is a faraway planet
The sun is as bright as a star
The sun is as light as a hammock
The sun is a very big star.

The sun is a romantic circle
That shines in the sky
The sun makes some of you
A little bit shy.

The sun is sunny so have a paddling pool out
But most of all really, I have no doubt
I love the sun.

Katie Thompson (7)
Linthorpe Community Primary School, Middlesbrough

Animals In Autumn

Squirrels running as fast as they can
Like a trapeze artist flying through the air.

Snails dawdling across a muddy pathway
Covered in a rainbow of colourful leaves.

Owls swooping
To catch their mini prey.

Hungry cemetery animals
Looking for conkers and acorns.

Perry Morgan (10)
Linthorpe Community Primary School, Middlesbrough

What Can I Be?

Ooh, ow, ouch, being hit by arrows is not very nice.
Where I am stored there's lots of mice.
I am used every day,
I can be held in every way.
Getting dents or holes,
Soldiers getting cold.
I can be red, orange and even blue,
When I saw the Celts I said, 'Who?'

What can I be?

Charlotte Jones (8)
Linthorpe Community Primary School, Middlesbrough

The Sun

The sun is a gigantic, orange fireball
The sun is your friend
The sun is a shiny, big star
The sun is a fire, flaming hot
The sun is a round, big circle
The sun is a romantic love heart
The sun is a sunset spreading around
The sun is a big ball
The sun is our light.

Hannah Scott (7)
Linthorpe Community Primary School, Middlesbrough

A Recipe For A Happy Classroom

First add a teaspoon of goodness,
A smiley teacher and room full of happiness,
Good lesson to bring you joy,
Kind people who are nice to you,
A teacher who is good at maths,
Next pour in good friends who are funny.

Lucy McCall (8)
Linthorpe Community Primary School, Middlesbrough

A Recipe For A Happy Classroom

Start off with a classroom
Add a bowlful of children,
Then add a pinch of friends.
Now add a dash of good behaviour,
Then rub together some kindness.
Next cook some funniness.
Now sprinkle some manners.
Stir in some bright and colourful displays
And last of all mix in some joy.

Amy Glazebrook (9)
Linthorpe Community Primary School, Middlesbrough

A Recipe For A Happy Classroom

Begin with a handful of friends,
Then stir in some bright colours.
Next take a bagful of joy,
After that add 100 grams of good behaviour.
An ounce of hard work just for good measure,
Then get a bowlful of books and pour it into the mixture.
To finish it off get a jug of funniness and kindness and pour it in
And that's a recipe for a happy classroom.

Joshua Young (8)
Linthorpe Community Primary School, Middlesbrough

A Happy Classroom

First get a spoonful of enjoyment.
After that get a tablespoon of children playing helpfully.
Next get a handful of children with laughter.
After that get a fin of a fish.
Next grab a handful of helpful children.
Next get a handful of children listening.
Finally hear the children play.

Kaleem Majid (8)
Linthorpe Community Primary School, Middlesbrough

A Recipe For A Happy Classroom

Begin with a classroom full of chairs and tables
And a smiling teacher for children to come in.
Then next come the kids giggling and talking.
Add a dash of work but especially listening well.
Fold in a spoonful of happy and joyful kids
And a sprinkle of manners and helpful things.
Kids watching fish in the dazzling tank.
A handful of bright, colourful pictures on the wall.
Soon they were going home
And saying bye-bye to their friends.

Laura Foster (8)
Linthorpe Community Primary School, Middlesbrough

A Recipe For A Happy Classroom

Begin with one hundred brilliant bags full of smiles,
This will make your classroom a happy place to learn.
Then sprinkle a little bit of laughter on
And then sprinkle a little bit of love on.
Mix it all together and carefully add a teaspoon of fun.
After that you must cook your recipe for three exciting hours.
Finally place your mixture into a bright and colourful classroom
With a smiling teacher
And don't forget to serve it all up with an aquarium full of fish.

Kennedy Smith Cassy (8)
Linthorpe Community Primary School, Middlesbrough

The Huge Tree

The huge tree is like a giant waving his arms against the
dusky sky.
Using his arms to push me away.
The falling leaves are like snowflakes falling swiftly from the
misty sky.
Grass blades tangle wildly as the autumn breeze blows.

Saffron Bowyer-Hogg (10)
Linthorpe Community Primary School, Middlesbrough

Cemetery

Creepy at night, you will get a fright,
Enormous graves, small graves,
You would want to be safe,
In your house with your mum and dad,
Spooky, hairy spiders climbing up your arm,
Sending bone-chilling shivers down your spine.

Multicoloured flowers that grow
Become bewitched and turn black at night
And the smell that comes about when the gates close is deadly.
Graves chattering,
Owls flying,
Squirrels leaping
In the cemetery.

Sara Cooper (10)
Linthorpe Community Primary School, Middlesbrough

The Cemetery

Conkers laying in the ground,
Waiting patiently to be found.
Squirrels run all around,
Looking for nuts on the ground.
Trees shivering in the breeze
And all the flowers stand next to leaves.

Knowing that they will be found,
The conkers lay all around.
Squirrels jumping across the floor,
Eating nuts and looking for more.
Tree skeletons wave their hands
At the passing by parade of bands.

Joshua Cassidy (10)
Linthorpe Community Primary School, Middlesbrough

Falling Leaves

Falling leaves are
Skating in the air
Landing anywhere they
Can find.
Falling leaves, red and
Brown on the floor
Make a cosy insect bed.
As the wind blows
The leaves jump like a
Frog springing on its back
Legs.
Falling leaves are sadly
Gone to find somewhere
Else to stay.

Megan McCullow (11)
Linthorpe Community Primary School, Middlesbrough

A Walk Through The Park

I can see . . .
Birds on branches,
Conkers on the floor.
Leaves falling off trees,
Floating to earth.
The leaves are changing,
They are now crispy.
It is cold as ice,
Yellow flowers growing.
The leaves are turning golden-brown and red,
Like a rainbow fading away.

Faisal Hussain (11)
Linthorpe Community Primary School, Middlesbrough

Leaves

Tall, twisty and bendy trees
Spiralling into the sky.
Leaves falling from the trees
On a cloudy, autumn day.
Landing with a soft bump,
Making a collection with
Ripe and shiny conkers,
Leaves and twigs.
Curled-up leaves under my feet,
Crunch like crispy nut cornflakes.
The wild branches swishing to and fro
In a beat to the wind
On one cloudy, autumn day.

Hayley McFarlane (10)
Linthorpe Community Primary School, Middlesbrough

Leaves

Leaves curled up
Balancing on the tips of the branches
Brown, crusty
Swishing leaves
Lying on the muddy floor.

Sunlight shining through the leaves
Like a jigsaw puzzle
Lying on the shadowy ground.
A carpet round the tree
Patterned by leaves and twigs.

Ryonni Daggett (10)
Linthorpe Community Primary School, Middlesbrough

The Cemetery

With autumn comes conkers,
Children going bonkers.
Brown and green conker shells fall
Down for all.

Squirrels run across the graves,
Like grey waves.
As they look for scraps to eat,
They jump and leap on their back feet.

All graves stand lonely,
They seem to say, 'If only . . .'
Gravestones conquered by mould
New and old.

The trees stand tall,
Watching their golden leaves swiftly fall.
Conkers drop like a rock thrown from the sky,
Smash, crack, then they die.

Philip James (10)
Linthorpe Community Primary School, Middlesbrough

A Walk

Through the cemetery I walk,
Leaves crunching underfoot.

The bare trees like skeletons,
Their arms and fingers moving in the wind.

Dead graves on the floor,
Beheaded, limbless statues as solid as metal.

Through the cemetery I walk,
Leaves crunching underfoot.

Richard Cowley (10)
Linthorpe Community Primary School, Middlesbrough

Squirrel

The graceful squirrel prances about
In the wild, untamed forest grass
Springing
Up and down
Up and down
Like a wave
On a stormy, winter's day.

The balancing squirrel climbs up
Tall, bended, twisted trees
Sits on the highest branches
Like a sculpture frozen for time
Spots its prey, gets ready.

Tail flicks
Chases and scoops
Like a ballerina dancing across the stage
An elegant performer.

Jack Boocock (11)
Linthorpe Community Primary School, Middlesbrough

The Cemetery

Birds chirping in the distance,
Wind swaying trees around,
Leaves crackling as they blow
Across the old, chipped gravestones.
Squirrels so elegant
As they scurry across the wild, emerald grass.
Conkers, mahogany-brown,
Shiny as a mirror ball.
Crows croaking as they rest
On the thin, twisted branches.

Katie Dixon (10)
Linthorpe Community Primary School, Middlesbrough

Autumn's Day

Dead leaves, crispy
And sticky
Lying curled up
On the ground
Leaves as rough
As sandpaper
Some with black
Spots on.

Leaves on the trees
Splashing together
Leaves blowing in
The wind like a man
Trying to keep his
Hat on.

Little creatures
Scurry away like
Children running
Around playing tig.
Trees spiral into
The sky like
A bird trying
To get its prey.

Chloe Jones (10)
Linthorpe Community Primary School, Middlesbrough

Tree

Tall, smooth, wavy, bendy tree
Swaying its branches in the air
Like a giant waving his hands
Inviting you into the woods.
The sounds of the leaves
Swishing in the wind
Bashing together.

Emma Hall (10)
Linthorpe Community Primary School, Middlesbrough

Crispy, Green Leaves

Crispy, green leaves
That crunch under my feet.
It sounds like empty
Packets of crisps
Scrunched up
Blowing swiftly on the muddy ground.
The wind grows and trees
Blow from side to side
While leaves fall
Safely on the ground.

Elena Durrani (10)
Linthorpe Community Primary School, Middlesbrough

The Scots Pine

A tree spiralling into the sky
As tall as Jack's beanstalk
Growing towards the door of the giant's castle.
Small, prickly leaves shaped like stars
Spread in clusters against a grey sky.
Leaves spiking the clouds as they go by.
A tree wrapped up in a rough, dark bark
Like a boy with a scarf around his neck on cold, autumn day.

Emily Hood (10)
Linthorpe Community Primary School, Middlesbrough

Varnished Conkers

Beautiful, brown conkers left on the moist, muddy floor,
Sitting like pebbles shimmering in the sunshine.
Look at the shell, spiky and green like a hedgehog's back.
Inside silky and soft where the conker lay.
The conker varnished and smooth on the top like woodgrain.
A picture of a horse's hoof.

Daniel Smith (10)
Linthorpe Community Primary School, Middlesbrough

The Cemetery

A dull, autumn day
Varnished, brown conkers
Dry, dead leaves
Sandy, cracked gravestones
Snapping long twigs
Delicate, tiny woodlice
Crawling under rough bark
A silky, smooth feather
Lying on muddy, soft ground.

Robert Ellis (10)
Linthorpe Community Primary School, Middlesbrough

Trees

Long, wild, twisted trees
Swaying in the autumn wind
Twigs like gigantic arms smashing together
Leaves twisting and turning wildly
The wind is howling
Trees are bending
With gigantic arms sweeping up the autumn leaves.

Anthony Snook (10)
Linthorpe Community Primary School, Middlesbrough

Twigs Snapping, Leaves Crackling

Twigs snap at the insects scuttling on the damp, spongy earth
While the leaves seem to crackle underfoot
Holding the grown earth down.

The wind blows making the leaves and twigs waltz, spin and whirl.
It's as if they are celebrating the cold, autumn's day.

Andrew North (10)
Linthorpe Community Primary School, Middlesbrough

The Cemetery

Leaves twisting
And turn wildly.
Crunching on the ground
Like delicate cornflakes.

Dead flowers that lie
On the muddy compost,
Bendy stem swaying
In the open, lighted sky.

Trees stand tall,
They feel rough
Wavy, bendy
And look as if
They are telling
Us something.

Lateef Owarth (10)
Linthorpe Community Primary School, Middlesbrough

Conker Tree

Tall, strong tree towering above the filthy soil,
Hundreds of conkers plunge
Like bombs falling from the sky.

Leaves blowing in the wind,
Seem to be flying,
Like the crows that can be heard,
Screeching in the distance.

Rough bark covers the mighty plant,
Seeing this admirable giant,
Inspired me to write this poem.

Scott David Rogers (10)
Linthorpe Community Primary School, Middlesbrough

The Cemetery Spook

Fallen gravestones lying dead
Each one a different colour
Conquered by mould
Beheaded statues, limbs amputated,
Yet still it lives.
Crows sit staring from the top
Of broken figures
Bare trees stand shivering in the wind
Crunching leaves lie underfoot,
Yet still it lives.

Elizabeth Devereux (11)
Linthorpe Community Primary School, Middlesbrough

Autumn Sounds

Leaves swishing and swaying from side to side
Like waves sliding up and down the sand.
A little squirrel scuttling on a tree
To knock the conkers down.
Leaves rustling in a strong breeze.
Cars humming up and down.
Little children playing games.
I like autumn because it's quiet and peaceful!

Faye Moore (10)
Linthorpe Community Primary School, Middlesbrough

Trees And Flowers

Walking in the cemetery
Finding trees and flowers
Red, blue, white, brown and green
Seeing squirrels jumping all round
We listen to the birds singing
We feel the crispy branches.

Helena Hussain (10)
Linthorpe Community Primary School, Middlesbrough

Cemetery In Autumn

Leaves are changing colours, red and crispy brown,
Drifting gracefully across the ground like models on the catwalk.
Shiny brown conkers as glistening as jewels
On the leafy, rustling ground.
The breeze hits softly against the autumn trees.

Grey squirrels scampering across the floor
Looking for the most perfect conker
Like a child searches for her mum.
It makes me happy to see autumn changes.

In the air a damp, leafy smell just like seeds turning,
Turning into flowers so sudden.
If you sit down for a moment
You know summer has turned into autumn.
New, gusty winds.
Autumn is here.

Amy Dixon (10)
Linthorpe Community Primary School, Middlesbrough

The Cemetery

Skin roughened like reptile skin
On the crispy, woodland floor.
New, shiny conkers
Nibbled by squirrels as they pass by.
Leaves crackling and crunching
As I stand on them.
When I walk between the gravestones
If I look up I see green leaves.
When I look down I see yellow leaves.

Sayeed Hussain Buksh (10)
Linthorpe Community Primary School, Middlesbrough

Cemetery

Leaves on the trees
Are turning yellow, brown
And red.
Cars beeping
Squirrels leaping
Conkers cracking open.

Crows squawking in the trees
Gravestones tumbling over
Statues beheaded with the weather
Flowers disappearing from here to there.

Paige Elizabeth Ferguson (10)
Linthorpe Community Primary School, Middlesbrough

The Wind

The wind blows through my hair
Like a brush
The wind passes through the trees
And makes the leaves fall
The wind picks up all the leaves
Off the cobbled floor
The wind blows the rain away
Like a broom sweeping the floor.

Charlotte Stoddart (10)
Linthorpe Community Primary School, Middlesbrough

Autumn - Haikus

Trees sway in the breeze
Autumn, beautiful in fall
Nature in beauty.

The world sings a song
The grass soon to make creatures
Trees, trees, trees are green.

Jasmine Thomas (9)
Linthorpe Community Primary School, Middlesbrough

The Cemetery

The crackle of crunchy leaves
Beneath my feet
I look up at the swaying trees
Branches almost bare.

Squirrels jumping off trees
Like a tide of waves.
People pass by, the squirrels freeze
Vanishing off like they were never there.

Fallen gravestones lying dead
Bunches of flowers around them.
Smooth, ripe conkers, shiny brown
Silky pebbles all over the ground.

Samaira Riaz (10)
Linthorpe Community Primary School, Middlesbrough

The Cemetery

Death is confusing for some I know,
Yet there is life in the land of the dead.
Trees are wrinkly, conkers rotten,
Sweet scents in the air,
But no flowers to be seen.
Conkers thrown like shooting stars,
But nothing to be seen.
Oh, what's this? Two squirrels scuttling up a tree
With more rotten conkers
But nothing, nothing else to be seen.
Death!
Life is short!

Marie Brown (11)
Linthorpe Community Primary School, Middlesbrough

Nature's Trail

Squirrels scurry round like lightning bolts
Their bush-like tails follow them in waves
They run round and round, up and down.

High and low birds fly swooping
A sweet tweet as they sit in the trees.

Scented flowers smell sassy
Bright petals and buzzy bees
The flowers sway in the breeze.

Thalia Bloundele (10)
Linthorpe Community Primary School, Middlesbrough

Cemetery

We take a stroll in the cemetery
With conkers brown as wood
Midnight climbing closer
Squirrels collecting nuts.

There are trees without leaves
They are scattered on the ground
Making a carpet of fire
For us to walk upon.

Imogen Ord-Smith (10)
Linthorpe Community Primary School, Middlesbrough

Conkers

They arrive in the autumn and depart in the spring.
They come in a shell that protects them
With its sharp, prickly grasp.
Boys and girls break them open.
They use them for battle and toughen them up.
Once smashed and broken they are left for dead.

Jordan Cane (10)
Linthorpe Community Primary School, Middlesbrough

The Park

Crispy leaves that crackle
Under my feet as I step
Quietly on the damp ground.

Glossy conkers as shiny as a polished shoe
Lay buried under crispy, brown leaves.

Tall, bendy trees spiral up to the sky
Allowing the rain to fall gently
As though they are giant umbrellas
Protecting me from the rain.

Lauren Boden (11)
Linthorpe Community Primary School, Middlesbrough

Happiness

Happiness is yellow like the sun burning in the sky
It sounds like the sea calming when it hits the sand
It feels like a squidge ball when it's burnt
It tastes like a big, fat beef burger made on the barbecue
It looks like a birthday cake waiting to be eaten
It smells like pepperoni pizza
It reminds me of Christmas.

Stefan Dezou (9)
Linthorpe Community Primary School, Middlesbrough

Autumn

Leaves crackling and crunching
Breaking up into segments,
Brown, twisted branches
Swaying about in the autumn breezes,
Conkers open from the spiky shells
Ready for a conker fight.

Lee Maskew (10)
Linthorpe Community Primary School, Middlesbrough

Nature

Varnished conkers
Like old furniture
Rolling out of their sharp, prickly,
Chestnut pod.
Slow snails on the hard, rough wood
Leaving a line of ooze.
Delicate woodlice on the moist soil
Like a miniature toy car wound up.
Branches roughened like reptile skin.
Ancient, crooked and sharp gravestones
Tilted like someone falling over.

Christopher Larkman (10)
Linthorpe Community Primary School, Middlesbrough

Squirrels

Squirrels scuttle, their tails
Follow behind like waves,
They scamper up and down
Tree trunks and along the ground.
Squirrels search high and low
For conkers and nuts,
When something moves they freeze
As still as statues,
Then dash as quick as a bullet
When something gets close.

Olivia Hood (10)
Linthorpe Community Primary School, Middlesbrough

Happiness

Happiness is bright yellow like the shining sun.
Happiness sounds like a singing bird in a tree.
Happiness smells like spring lilies in the garden.
Happiness tastes like fresh, juicy apples.
Happiness feels like a soft, fluffy pillow.
Happiness looks like a laughing child.
Happiness reminds me of playing out in the sun.

Amey Sanders
Marton Grove Primary School, Middlesbrough

Happiness

Happiness tastes like eating a juicy, green apple.
Happiness feels like cuddling a soft, furry teddy.
Happiness is blue like the twinkling sky on a summer's day.
Happiness looks like the bright sun shining in the sky.
Happiness smells like chocolate being melted.
Happiness sounds like a red robin carolling on a winter's morning.
Happiness reminds me of a hot bath filled with bubbles.

Sophie Jinks (10)
Marton Grove Primary School, Middlesbrough

Love

Love is pink like a soft, melting marshmallow.
Love feels like a fluffy, white cloud.
Love tastes like a bar of melting chocolate.
Love looks like bubbles floating in the air.
Love smells like a flowering rose in a garden.
Love sounds like a bird singing in the warm sunshine.
Love reminds me of a bubbling jacuzzi on a sunny day.

Lauren Wilson (10)
Marton Grove Primary School, Middlesbrough

Love

Love is red like a juicy apple.
Love tastes like freshly-picked strawberries.
Love smells like the scent of a rose.
Love looks like two pieces of liquorice joined together.
Love reminds me of my family.
Love feels like a warm, furry cushion.
Love sounds like a bird singing in the sun.

Emma Clare (10)
Marton Grove Primary School, Middlesbrough

Fear

Fear feels like I'm never going to be happy again.
Fear tastes like biting into a sour lemon that dries up my throat.
Fear is black like a threatening cloud taking over the sky.
Fear looks like a black bat chasing after people.
Fear sounds like a big bass drum banging in my head.
Fear smells like a rotten tomato that never goes away.
Fear reminds me of a huge, hairy spider clutching onto my leg.

Harry William Drake (10)
Marton Grove Primary School, Middlesbrough

Love

Love is red like a hot, blazing fire.
Love tastes like melting marshmallows in your mouth.
Love feels like a warm, fluffy, hot-water bottle.
Love smells like fresh roses.
Love looks like a beating, red-hot heart.
Love sounds like a thudding in your body.
Love reminds me of a jacuzzi of bubbly, hot water.

Kelsey Morris (10)
Marton Grove Primary School, Middlesbrough

Laughter

Laughter is blue like the deep, dark, wavy oceans.
Laughter sounds like young men at a stag night.
Laughter tastes like a fresh packet of McCoy's Thai Sweet
Chicken crisps.
Laughter smells like freshly-cooked sausages.
Laughter looks like the sun starting to set.
Laughter feels like a soft, squidgy pillow.
Laughter reminds me of the birth of my baby brother.

Connor Richardson (10)
Marton Grove Primary School, Middlesbrough

Boredom

Boredom is grey like a developing cold cloud.
Boredom looks like a park fading away.
Boredom feels like a pair of eyes staring and watching.
Boredom tastes like chewing and munching on a raw potato.
Boredom sounds like spiders' cobwebs swishing around.
Boredom reminds me of a plain, empty room.

Lewis Paul Thompson (10)
Marton Grove Primary School, Middlesbrough

Love

Love is red like a racing heart.
Love sounds like a beautiful, singing nightingale.
Love looks like a brightly shining sun.
Love feels like a tingling touch.
Love reminds me of my family.
Love smells like a giant rose swishing in the air.
Love tastes like beautiful ice cream.

Sophie Batey (10)
Marton Grove Primary School, Middlesbrough

Laughter

Laughter sounds like sweet birds singing songs.
Laughter is blue like a light sky changing shape.
Laughter tastes like sparkling lemonade.
Laughter smells like perfume.
Laughter looks like two jolly men having beer.
Laughter feels like your heart's beating.
Laughter reminds me of April Fool's Day.

Daniel Chirnside (10)
Marton Grove Primary School, Middlesbrough

Fear

Fear is black like clinging, dusty, old curtains.
Fear sounds like loud footsteps on the landing.
Fear tastes like red-hot sweets.
Fear smells like a hot, boiling fireball.
Fear looks like a cat dying.
Fear feels like fire burning on my hot, bony spine.
Fear reminds me of coal melting in a crackling fire.

Jade Frost (11)
Marton Grove Primary School, Middlesbrough

Boredom

Boredom is plain like a white sheet of paper waiting.
Boredom tastes like a sweaty bone which has been chewed by a dog.
Boredom feels like cold water running down a spine.
Boredom looks like drying paint.
Boredom sounds like an endless rain dripping from a roof.
Boredom smells like a pair of swaying, dull curtains.
Boredom reminds me of a smelly bed sheet.

Lewis Wigham (10)
Marton Grove Primary School, Middlesbrough

Fear, Love, Hate And Happiness

Fear is white like a chilling, evil ghost.
It sounds like howling, screaming wind.
It smells like rotten, putrid air.
It feels like a tingling, stabbing pain.

Love is pink like a fluffy, heart-shaped pillow.
It sounds like violins and angels.
It smells like dark red roses and chocolate.

Hate is blue like a shark speeding through the ice-cold sea.
It sounds like long nails screeching down the blackboard.
It smells like grey, thick smoke.

Happiness is yellow like a warm, sunny day.
It sounds like birds singing and children laughing.
It smells like sweet spring flowers.

Robert Daniel Harman (10)
Marton Grove Primary School, Middlesbrough

Shrek

Your ears are like candles.
Your teeth are like a knife.
Your tummy is fat like a cake.
Your face is like a ball.
Your lips are like green beans.
Your eyes are like cherries.
Your arms are like charging knights.
Your legs are like tree trunks.

Faisal Mohammed, Christopher Dillon, Akbar Arshad (11),
Sean Laver, Sophie Spence & Kirsty Veitch (12)
Priory Woods Special School, Middlesbrough

My Family

First it goes my sister
She is Scooby-Doo mad
But when I turn it off
She gets very sad.

Then comes my mum
She is the queen of the house
Whenever I am naughty
She shrieks like a mouse.

Now it is my dad
He thinks he's the boss
But when I tell him that
He gets very cross.

And here comes my nana
She walks everywhere
She always has lots of bags
And handles them with care.

Now it is me Jessica Seale
I am rather lazy
But the best thing about me
Is I am Busted crazy.

Jessica Seale (8)
St Clare's RC Primary School, Acklam

Autumn - Haikus

Leaves dropping off trees.
The leaves are falling off trees.
The rain is so strong.

Conkers drop from trees.
You can smell it in the breeze.
Wrap up warm today.

Collecting conkers
We search for them everywhere.
The leaves on the ground.

Dominic Ragusa (10)
St Clare's RC Primary School, Acklam

My Family

Here is my dad
Sometimes crazy
He cleans up a lot
But sometimes he can be lazy.

Meet my mum
She's fresh as a bun
She always takes me out
And we have lots of fun.

Along comes Adam
Creepy as mice
Tells me what he does
He eats chicken and rice.

Next there's Grandma
White as snow
She always does a pose
And shows off her big, red bow.

And here comes my grandpa
He is very funny
Because he is so funny
He hops like a bunny.

Then here comes me
Fresh as home-made tea
I like eating fish
I buzz around like a buzzy bee.

Now here comes my family
Precious to me
What can I do without them?
They are as lovable as can be.

Tessa Molly Anna Stobbs (8)
St Clare's RC Primary School, Acklam

My Family

This is my dad
Taller than a tree
As sharp as a needle
As strong as can be.

Here's my little sister
She's as sharp as a tusk
As clever as a scientist
As dirty as the dust.

Here's my brother, he's as tall as can be
He's football crazy
As quick as a shark
But he's so very lazy.

Here's my mum
As small as can be
 As quick as a cheetah
And she's just like me.

Here's my sister
She's as mad as can be
She's as sharp as a pencil
And stronger than a tree.

Stephen Connors (8)
St Clare's RC Primary School, Acklam

Autumn - Haikus

The rain drops quickly.
The rain drops on the windows.
The rain drops all day.

Conkers fall off trees.
The animals hibernate.
The leaves fall off trees.

The leaves change colours.
It gets dark very early.
It's always frosty.

Taylor Middleton (9)
St Clare's RC Primary School, Acklam

My Niece Millie

My niece Millie
Is princess crazy
She loves them so much
That she's sometimes lazy.

My niece Millie
Is very kind
She's very happy
And sometimes loses her mind.

My niece Millie
Is like a bunny
She bounces all the time
And is very funny.

My niece Millie
Is as beautiful as a rose
She's very, very pretty
And she's got smelly toes.

Kathryn Clarke (8)
St Clare's RC Primary School, Acklam

My Family

Introducing my mam, she's . . .
As kind as a queen
Or funky as a monkey
She's never, ever mean.

Next is my dad
He's as cool as a dude
As messy as Tessy
And never, ever rude.

My brother Jake
Is as great as a queen
Never, ever naughty
Never, ever mean.

Luke Symmonds (8)
St Clare's RC Primary School, Acklam

My Family

This is my dad
He is football mad
When we lose the football
He is so sad.

This is my mum
My mum loves to clean
But when everything is messy
She is very mean.

This is Michael
Michael is my brother
He calls my mum
Mother.

My brother Danny
Is as handsome as a prince
He loves maths
And he smells fresh as mints.

This is my nanna
She loves to shop
For important things
But she calls my grandad a mop.

Moly Sherwood (8)
St Clare's RC Primary School, Acklam

Autumn - Haikus

Wind whistling through trees,
Blown leaves rustling on the ground,
Conkers on the floor.

Orange and brown leaves,
Big leaves crackle on the floor,
I jump in the leaves.

Luciano Rossi (9)
St Clare's RC Primary School, Acklam

Mum And Dad

Here's my mum
She's as clean as can be
She's as pretty as a fairy
And she likes a cup of tea.

Here's my dad
He's football mad
But if he loses
He is so, so sad.

Here's my mum
She's small as could be
She is kind like the Queen
And she likes to be at the sea.

Here's my dad
He's as strong as a tree
He's as handsome as the king
And looks like a buzzy bee.

Josh Hutchinson (8)
St Clare's RC Primary School, Acklam

My Family

My mum is as nice as can be
We are music mad
She watches football
When we lose she is sad.

Me and my dad are football mad
He loves to take a bath
He says stuff
That makes me laugh.

My brother is game mad
He is so funny
He is like a fluffy cloud
He reminds of a bunny.

Oliver Hughes (8)
St Clare's RC Primary School, Acklam

My Cousin Dan

My cousin Dan
Is motorbike mad
But when he loses
He's a little sad.

My cousin Dan
Is sometimes very loud
He's always smart
And he makes us very proud.

My cousin Dan
Is very good at art
He's as strong as a building
And has hair like Bart.

My cousin Dan
Is a little bit lazy
He's a little bit cheeky
And he's motorbike crazy.

Jordan Hood (8)
St Clare's RC Primary School, Acklam

My Dad

First here's my dad
He is very lazy
When we score a goal
He goes very crazy.

Dad is sometimes very kind
And he is smelly too
He has got a kind mind
And just one pair of shoes.

When my dad goes out
He is as clean as could be
He never dares to shout
And he is taller than a tree.

Hannah Crackell (8)
St Clare's RC Primary School, Acklam

The White Family

This is my mum
She loves to sing
Every day
Ring, ring, ring.

This is my dad
He always shouts
Run, run, running
Always dashing about.

This is Angela
She is very nice
Always very happy
And she loves mice.

This is Brendan
He is very lazy
Never very helpful
But is football crazy.

This is Frances
She is very kind
She is not tidy
Because she hasn't got much of a mind.

This is my gran,
She is very nice
Always very healthy
But is not keen on rice.

This is my grandad
He's as tall as a tree
Always helping everyone
Especially me.

Now I have to go
I felt a rumble in my belly
It's now my lunchtime
And I'm having purple jelly.

Katie White (8)
St Clare's RC Primary School, Acklam

My Family Poem

Here's my dad
He's very good at art
But he's also sport mad
He dresses smart to look the part.

Here's my mum
She's very kind
But certainly not dumb
And she's got a great mind.

Here's my brother
He's taller than a tree
He's bigger than his grandmother
And he hates the cheese called brie.

Here's me
I take after my dad
I also drink tea
And I'm sport mad.

Here's my grandad
He's very, very lazy
I've never seen him act bad
But he's football crazy.

Jonathan James Coleby (9)
St Clare's RC Primary School, Acklam

Autumn - Haikus

Leaves have come off trees
Tangling up in my laces
The leaves are dark brown.

Climbing up bare trees
Lots of thin branches have snapped
We collect conkers.

Playing on my bike
Outside with all of my friends
Having lots of fun.

Emily Callaghan (9)
St Clare's RC Primary School, Acklam

My Brother

My brother is as sound as a train
Laughs like a bear
And as handsome as can be
He always likes to dare.

My brother always likes to play
On a sunny day
He is always messy
And always plays on a sunny day.

Here's my brother, he is always funny
He always plays
Acts like a three-year-old
On a nice, sunny Sunday day.

My brother is dozy
Is football crazy
He likes to play
And is always lazy.

Nicole Richmond (8)
St Clare's RC Primary School, Acklam

My Sister Millie

This is my sister Millie
She is cheeky as a monkey
She gets on my nerves
And watches me very sneakily.

This is my sister
She is very cute
She plays with her toys
And she plays the flute.

This is my sister
She is very funny
She hops on one leg
Because she's a funny bunny.

Nicole Pritchard (8)
St Clare's RC Primary School, Acklam

My Crazy Family

Katie, Katie, my cousin Katie
She's really very kind
When it was my birthday
She got my favourite card and her name was signed.

This is my mum
She's really funny
She jumps up and down
Like a bunny.

Here's my dad
He's really very fat
But when he sees a furry thing
He goes very mad and it's a cat.

Introducing the Kuby family
That are all very nice
When we go to the shops to buy something
Before we buy we check the price.

Meet my aunty, my aunty Anne
She's incredibly kind as could be
When I'm thirsty
She gives me lemonade to drink.

Here's my grandpa, a very nice one too
And as clean as could be
When I am upset
He comforts me.

This is my pet, my hamster
She crawled up my mum's leg
And when she died
I couldn't get her out of my head.

Helen Kathleen Kuby (8)
St Clare's RC Primary School, Acklam

My Big Cousin Michael

My big cousin is very lazy
My big cousin is football crazy
My big cousin is very messy
My big cousin has a friend called Bessy.

My big cousin has lots of friends
My big cousin always bends
My big cousin is school mad
My big cousin has a massive dad.

My big cousin is as tall as a tree
My big cousin is kind to me
My big cousin is as funny as clown
My big cousin never has a frown.

My big cousin squeals like a mouse
My big cousin is nearly always in the house
My big cousin is as strong as a Viking
My big cousin acts like my king.

My big cousin is as clean as a medal
My big cousin is as handsome as a treble
My big cousin is as fast as a cheetah
My big cousin is a meat eater.

Hayley Nicholas (8)
St Clare's RC Primary School, Acklam

Autumn - Haikus

The leaves are falling
Lots of colours everywhere
I stamp on them all.

I jump in the leaves
The leaves make rustling noises
It is lots of fun.

The morning is dark
I always slip on the leaves
I really like it.

Daniel Hyde (9)
St Clare's RC Primary School, Acklam

My Sister

Introducing my sister Dion
She is like a queen
She is posh like a queen
She is never mean.

My sister Dion
She is kind
She's as kind as an 11-year-old
Sometimes loses her mind.

My sister Dion
She is lazy
She snoozes a lot too
She is so dog crazy.

My sister Dion
She is strong as a gorilla
She loves picking me up
She loves watching thrillers.

My sister Dion
She is a cheeky monkey
That's her favourite animal
And she is funky.

My sister Dion
She is smart
She is smarter than a teacher
She has a lovely heart.

Jacy Yates (8)
St Clare's RC Primary School, Acklam

My Family

Here is my dad
He's taller than a tree
He's PlayStation crazy
And is funny as can be.

Here is my mum
She is very funny
She is so kind, she lets my friends come and play
My mum is as happy as a bunny.

Here is my brother
He's as silly as a clown
He's as small as a mouse
He wears my mum's dressing gown.

Here are my cousins
Big, tall and small
They all like horses
And two of them like football.

Here is my cat
Her colour is tortoiseshell
She sleeps on my mat
When she was on the garage, she fell.

Sarah Connor (8)
St Clare's RC Primary School, Acklam

My Family Poem

Now here is my dad
He likes stars
He also likes planets
He wants to fly to Mars!

Here is my mum
Nicer than some
Baking and making
Yes, that's my mum!

Here is my grampa
He is brill
With a cup of tea
And a tummy to fill.

Here is my brother
Taller than a tree
He is called Chris
He's kind as can be.

Next is my pet
He is a dog
He loves chewing
Hard, brown logs.

Next is me
I am clever and funny
I like sweets
But I don't like honey.

Now all of the family
Put together
Clever and funny
Will last forever!

Lucy McElhone (8)
St Clare's RC Primary School, Acklam

Autumn - Haikus

Leaves falling off trees,
Leaves turn golden, cover paths,
They lie on the ground.

Conkering time now,
Conker shells, hollow inside,
I collect them all.

Bonfire Night is great,
It is my brother's birthday,
Fireworks lighting.

Pumpkins outside gates,
Scary faces at the door,
People give you sweets.

Sarah Louise Price (9)
St Clare's RC Primary School, Acklam

Autumn - Haikus

Autumn time is here
Golden leaves falling off trees
Hear conkers smashing.

Conkering is here
Conkers getting collected
The event is here.

Fires big and burning
Sparklers all round tonight
Laughter everywhere.

Animals hiding
Collecting food for winter
Never to be seen.

Jade McElwee (9)
St Clare's RC Primary School, Acklam

All Four Seasons - Haikus

Pink blossom on trees
The sun is sometimes shining
Let's go out and play.

The birds are singing
Flowers have started to bloom
We are all happy.

Now the sun is hot
We play out in the garden
Playing in the sun.

In the summertime
The sky's brilliantly blue
And I'm having fun.

It is autumn now
Hallowe'en is in autumn
Dark nights are coming.

The sun is going
The nights are getting colder
Weather's changing now.

Snow is on its way
Christmas is nearly here now
We are excited.

Playing in the snow
Sending letters to Santa
Now it's Christmas time.

Katy McHugh (9)
St Clare's RC Primary School, Acklam

Autumn - Haikus

Golden leaves falling
Dropping in the stream below
Lying there floating.

Conkers collected
The big event was smashing!
Conkers scattering.

Fire, hot and burning,
Bonfire Night, it is here now,
Guy Fawkes burning bright.

Animals hiding,
Hibernating for winter,
All cosy, sleeping.

Beth Knight (9)
St Clare's RC Primary School, Acklam

Autumn - Haikus

Leaves falling off trees,
With the freezing autumn breeze,
Leaves crunch under feet.

Conkers collected,
Let's all play conkers, who'll win?
Hear conkers smashing.

Bonfire Night is fun!
Guy Fawkes burning here tonight,
Fireworks spark tonight.

Animals prepare,
For hibernation today,
They'll sleep for some months.

Sarah Mitchell (9)
St Clare's RC Primary School, Acklam

The Four Seasons - Haikus

The sun is shining,
Pink and flowery blossom,
Let's go out and play.

The flowers have grown,
It is very warm today,
The birds are singing.

I am scorching hot,
The sun is getting hotter,
Do you want to play?

Playing in the sun,
Come on, let's go to the park,
It is summertime.

Now it is autumn,
We collect all the conkers,
All the leaves have gone.

We all wrap up warm,
The chestnuts fall off the tree,
The trees are all bare.

The snow is now here,
We all have to wrap up warm,
Christmas is coming.

All the sun has gone,
We will all play with the snow,
Let's go play snow fights.

Chloe Meehan (9)
St Clare's RC Primary School, Acklam

The Four Seasons - Haikus

Spring:
Springtime is now here
All the leaves back on the trees
We all like the spring.

Lots of pink blossom
There are lots of little lambs
And lots of cute chicks.

Summer:
In the summertime
People go on holiday
Lovely, cool ice cream.

The sun is shining
It is getting hotter now
Not a lot of rain.

Autumn:
We like the autumn
Leaves are falling off the trees
Brown, red and golden.

Rustling all the time
Running through the big, long park
In the autumn days.

Winter:
Lots of lovely snow
Lots of angels on the ground
Snowmen all around.

We are very cold
We sit next to the warm fire
Stay inside to play.

Jenny Linsley (9)
St Clare's RC Primary School, Acklam

Autumn - Haikus

There is always rain
The drops are on the window
It is always wet.

You can smell the breeze
You can smell the autumn breeze
My friends smell the breeze.

Do you like autumn?
I like autumn the best now
I like the autumn.

I like the conkers
You can go conker picking
I love the conkers.

Peter F Martin (10)
St Clare's RC Primary School, Acklam

Autumn - Haikus

The conkers are big,
The leaves are big and shiny,
The leaves are falling.

Walking in the leaves,
The leaves are big on the floor,
Crunching on the floor.

Wind whistling quite loud,
It blows dust in the distance,
It can hurt your eyes.

I love the conkers,
You can go conker picking,
Whose is the biggest?

Richard John Martin (9)
St Clare's RC Primary School, Acklam

The Four Seasons - Haikus

Spring
> Birds are on the trees
> Little chicks, calves, birds are born
> The nights are brighter.

> Warmer every day
> Flowers are starting to grow
> Blossom on the trees.

Summer
> It is very warm
> Lollies melt in the hot sun
> Children playing out.

> Sizzling barbecues
> Sausage in a breaded bun
> Burgers smell lovely.

Autumn
> Raindrops are falling
> Leaves are falling off the trees
> Chestnut shells falling.

> Trees are sticks and twigs
> Leaves are golden brown and red
> Dark nights every night.

Winter
> It is very cold
> Snow drops, falling from the sky
> It is very white.

> Now building snowmen
> Children having snowball fights
> Icy roads about.

Ellie Clarke (10)
St Clare's RC Primary School, Acklam

The Four Seasons - Haikus

Spring
The sun is shining
In the garden flowers bloom
Let's go out and play.

It is the springtime
It is very warm today
The birds are singing.

Summer
The summer is here
The leaves on the trees are green
The tree trunk is brown.

It is very hot
The sun is getting hotter
It's too hot to play.

Autumn
The leaves are falling
Let's go and collect conkers
They are nice and brown.

The leaves are falling
The chestnut shells are growing
They are nice and round.

Winter
The snow is falling
We have to wrap up warmly
To play in the snow.

All the sun has gone
We will have to play with snow
Let's play with the snow.

Ross Young (9)
St Clare's RC Primary School, Acklam

Autumn - Haikus

Leaves drop from the trees
Raindrops go on the windows
The rain's powerful.

Conkers in autumn
You can go conker picking
The wind is blowing.

It is cool today
Animals all hibernate
Crunchy leaves fall down.

Smooth, green leaves changing
You can smell cold in the breeze
The wind blows through trees.

Luke Allen (10)
St Clare's RC Primary School, Acklam

Autumn

Leaves are falling down,
Covering your garden wall,
With every colour.

Bouncing off my head,
Blowing all around the park,
Red, brown and golden.

On Bonfire Night,
Leaves crackling within the fire,
Burning to pieces.

Gather up the leaves,
And throw them up in the air,
They glide slowly down.

Harriet Glence (9)
St Clare's RC Primary School, Acklam

The Four Seasons - Haikus

Spring is the season
Going on to the summer
It is nice weather.

There are animals
It is quite a nice, warm day
Flowers are blooming.

The sun is glowing
In the summer it is warm
People sunbathing.

Eating nice burgers
People having barbecues
Sausage in a bun.

Now there are conkers
The leaves are very crunchy
It's quite cold today.

It's starting to rain
Everybody is so cold
The weather is bad.

Now it is winter
The snow is on the pavement
It is so freezing.

I throw a snowball
And I make a big snowman
Let's play with the snow.

In one whole, big year
Three hundred sixty-five days
Drinking hot chocolate.

Michael James Bythway (9)
St Clare's RC Primary School, Acklam

Four Seasons - Haikus

Summer
It was really hot
I ate a lot of ice cream
Bees and wasps buzz by.

In the summertime
The sky was brilliant blue
The sun was shining.

Spring
Springtime is now here
The leaves are all golden brown
Nights are getting bright.

It is really dark
Animals are being born
It starts to get warm.

Autumn
Silk inside chestnuts
Autumn days, the grass is jewelled
Conkers fall off trees.

The grass is soggy
Leaves change from green to dark gold
Flowers are dying.

Winter
It is very cold
The snow falls from the dark sky
I play in my house.

I can make snowmen
Children enjoy snowball fights
They keep themselves warm.

Kate Hilton (9)
St Clare's RC Primary School, Acklam

Seasons - Haikus

The autumn season,
Leaves are falling off the trees,
They lie on the ground.

The winter season,
Make a snowman very tall,
And fight in the snow.

It's the spring season,
And lambs jump through the long grass,
Baby lambs are born.

The summer season,
I play out till darkness falls,
It is very warm.

It is Bonfire Night,
The sky is full of sparkles,
We set off fireworks.

I like some warm soup,
We might be getting presents,
When Santa Claus comes.

Barbecues in spring,
The corn and grass grow in spring,
It's the end of spring.

Parties in summer,
It is as hot as the sun,
Drinking lemonade.

Tom Driscoll (9)
St Clare's RC Primary School, Acklam

Autumn - Haikus

Leaves are falling down,
Leaves are turning golden brown,
Chestnuts are falling.

All snug in your bed,
Hot porridge waiting downstairs,
A hot cup of tea.

The fire burning,
Sitting in front of the fire,
Nights are getting dark.

It's getting so cold,
Birds are flying to the west,
The sun is not out.

Children are laughing,
When you're in your warm, warm bed,
The kettle's boiling.

Deanna Parry (9)
St Clare's RC Primary School, Acklam

A Rainy Autumn - Haikus

The rain pours on us.
We wear coats to block the wind.
The rain wets the floor.

The conkers fall off the trees.
The leaves start to fall below.
Animals make beds.

Rain wets the windows.
Conkers fall on people's heads.
Children play outside.

Leaves are everywhere.
Rain falls and waters the plants.
The wind blows the trees.

Charlie Collin (9)
St Clare's RC Primary School, Acklam

Autumn - Haikus

Leaves are falling down
They lie on the path below
Leaves are brown and gold.

It will be winter
People are finding conkers
It will be Christmas.

I have got presents
The weather is getting cold
The snow is melting.

The children laughing
I can smell the barbecues
It is summer soon.

Luke Bollands (9)
St Clare's RC Primary School, Acklam

Autumn - Haikus

Leaves falling from trees.
The leaves are as green as grass.
The wind is so strong.

The sun is quite hot.
The weather is quite normal.
Outside with my friends.

Climbing up big trees.
Cats playing with cotton balls.
Animals playing.

Animals eating.
People stamping in the rain.
People playing ball.

Louis Stobbs (9)
St Clare's RC Primary School, Acklam

Seasons - Haikus

Slowly leaves fall down
The wind whispers to the leaves
Silently they fall.

Conkers very brown
Then they fall onto the ground
The animals sleep.

The cold is coming
The snow is as cold as ice
People are cold too.

We all love the snow
Snow is as white as cotton
It is dark at night.

In spring chicks hatch out
The blossom is on the tree
The sun is shining.

People are walking
The sky is as bright as fire
Children play outside.

People at the sea
The sun's as bright as the stars
People eat ice cream.

Children have great fun
Children play beside the lake
People sit outside.

Chloe Tempestoso (9)
St Clare's RC Primary School, Acklam

Autumn - Haikus

Dew on the treetops
Some brown chestnuts on the ground
Brown leaves in my shoes.

Climbing up the trees
Reaching for the conker shells
Chucking bad away.

Collecting firewood
The burning fire in my face
Time to blow it out.

Collecting some food
Squirrels running around trees
Animals hiding.

Jessica McKinley (9)
St Clare's RC Primary School, Acklam

Summertime

Summertime the weather is fine,
And adults have barbecues and wine,
Little children play in paddling pools,
As the older ones go to school,
In the summertime.

The birds are singing a happy, a happy tune,
And all the flowers are in bloom,
Melting ice cream in your hand,
As you play in the sand,
In the summertime.

People play on the beach,
The sea within easy reach,
Adults chill out in the sun,
Watching children having fun,
In the summertime.

Sarah Pinkney (11)
St Mark's Elm Tree Primary School, Fairfield

Teacher Weather Forecast

Starting off shiny and sunny
Come to the afternoon
Mrs Coe is like a storm
And starts pouring down.

Mrs Munns starts off sunny and breezy
And by the afternoon she starts spitting
And then goes into a storm.

Sunny at the start
And always a bright star
Mrs Leek stays the same all day.

Always happy and smiling
But when it comes to the afternoon
Sometimes a big storm starts.

My mum is sunny
And shines like a huge star
But can go into a storm.

Ryan Todd (10)
St Mark's Elm Tree Primary School, Fairfield

Moving School

I worry about secondary school
New people, new friends
Will they like me?
Gang up on me?
New people, new teachers
Will they like me?
Support me?
New work, new lessons
Will I manage it?
Get good grades?
I worry about secondary school.

Charlotte McCann (10)
St Mark's Elm Tree Primary School, Fairfield

Lost Alone

Lost alone, all alone,
Never, ever found.

I entered the supermarket,
Squeezing Mum's hand,
I heard a call,
And turned around.

Nobody was there,
I looked for my mum,
But she was . . . where?
I was lost. I started to cry.

Lost alone, all alone,
Never, ever found.

Then I noticed, this man was looking solemnly,
He muttered, 'What's the matter?
There's no need to make that clatter.
Don't worry, I'll find your mum.'

He led me up to my mum,
Through aisles and aisles,
I ran to her and squeezed her tight,
She muttered, 'Everything will be alright.'

Lost alone, all alone,
Never, ever found.

I walked out of the supermarket,
Squeezing my mum's hand,
Glad to be back with her,
Walking hand in hand.

Lost alone, all alone,
Now I'm loved and found.

Rachel Hartley (10)
St Mark's Elm Tree Primary School, Fairfield

My Sister Faye

My sister is a baby
Her hair is very crazy
Faye tries to walk.

When Faye crawls
She drives you up the walls
Faye likes doggies
But she doesn't like moggies.

When Faye is at someone's house
She squeaks like a mouse
Faye says, 'Dada.'
She also says, 'Baba.'

Lauren Rodgers (10)
St Mark's Elm Tree Primary School, Fairfield

Dragons

Dragons are fierce
Big and small
Lazy and fat
Cute and tall.

Dragons are green
Red and black
Blue or purple
With a broken back.

Dragons are cute
When they hatch
In their eggs
They need to learn how to catch.

Christopher Scott (10)
St Mark's Elm Tree Primary School, Fairfield

Lonely

I am all alone
It's my first day at school
My mam has gone and left me
What am I to do?

Have I got three heads?
Everybody is looking at me
Don't they know my heart is heavy?
I wish someone would help me.

Daniel Boston (11)
St Mark's Elm Tree Primary School, Fairfield

Mountains

Mountains are such funny things
I wonder how they're made?
They seem to pop out of nowhere.
Their tops always there.
Over 1100 mountains, they are very high.
Always getting bigger and never stopping.

Phillip Rowe (9)
St Mark's Elm Tree Primary School, Fairfield

The Victim

How come I get bullied?
I hate coming to school,
They call my family names,
They beat me up.
    I have no friends,
    I'm scared to tell anyone.

Claire Stephenson (10)
St Mark's Elm Tree Primary School, Fairfield

The Music Machine

My music makes me feel relaxed and happy,
I hate cars, they don't make me wacky,
My music makes me in a mood
Which I wish I was in all the time,
The music makes me think about my friends,
The music is cool, relaxing and enjoyable,
My music sounds fast and slow,
I hate hip-hop music, it isn't something I'm into,
I love my music, it is my life,
I can imagine myself laying on a beach
With my music surrounding me,
My music is also like the cinema
Because I like the cinema and music,
My music makes me feel relaxed,
I hate rap music, it's abusive,
My music is my life,
My music is my friend,
Thank you, music, you're the best.

Bethany Riley (10)
St Mark's Elm Tree Primary School, Fairfield

Depression In Words

She climbed out from her cosy bed,
Feeling bright as gold,
But when she looked into the mirror,
She began to feel old,
For as it came as such a shock,
Her image went up in flames,
And for all the things that ever happened,
She felt she had the blame.

In the form of ashes,
She fell to the floor,
To live the life of the Devil,
For eternity and more.

Rebecca Moira Bean (10)
St Mark's Elm Tree Primary School, Fairfield

The Life Of Stan

There's a boy who stares at the chair,
He has wavy, brown hair,
When it starts to rain,
He feels no pain,
He doesn't have a single friend,
His sadness doesn't seem to end.

He has a friend now,
And he controls the bow
Of a ship, grand and high,
It almost touches the sky.

Now he is an old man,
He still remembers the sea,
I'm his grandson, yes, that's me,
My grandad is called Stan,
So now that he is old,
There are many stories to be told.

Ryan Morgan (11)
St Mark's Elm Tree Primary School, Fairfield

Dragons

Dragons are mythical beasts,
That may have walked our Earth,
Long ago.

They could breathe fire,
Well, that's how the tale goes.
Also they could fly over blue skies.

Some could breathe ice,
And freeze unworthy knights,
Well, that's how the tale goes.

Ryan Harwood (11)
St Mark's Elm Tree Primary School, Fairfield

Italy

I have had a trip to Italy,
It was really cool,
They say, 'Ciao,' to say hi,
And, 'Si' for yes.

I went to the beach,
The sea laps on the pure sand,
It's boiling hot so you can barely stand!
It's great fun for me!

I love the place
And all its sights
It's so cool and hot too
They have lots of shops.

Italy is the best!
Come and visit
It's better than all the rest!
You won't want to leave.

Cara Barugh (10)
St Mark's Elm Tree Primary School, Fairfield

Lost

I was lost in the playground
With kids running round and round
I felt lonely
And left out
I stood on the wall
Day after day
Waiting
For people to make friends
With me
One day
A new pupil came to our school
And stood next to me
On the wall.

Ryan Bennett (10)
St Mark's Elm Tree Primary School, Fairfield

The New Boy

He sits and stares,
Looking at the happy children playing.
The other children play,
Running, skipping, jumping.
He just sits there,
Sad, looking, hoping
For a friend to come.
All he does is sit there
Day after day.
Every day that passes
His sadness grows.
The fear in his eyes
Is strong.

Alexander Kitching (10)
St Mark's Elm Tree Primary School, Fairfield

Trees Are Great

Trees are great
They stand up straight
And they drop leaves on your head.
When it snows
They bounce snowballs back at you.

So answer me please
If there weren't any trees
Where would owls sleep?
Where would the children get shade?
Where would squirrels hide their nuts?
What would dogs lie under?

Adam Melville (8)
St Mark's Elm Tree Primary School, Fairfield

Playgrounds

Playgrounds are such fun places,
Know what I mean?
Everyone seems to run, jump, talk
And do cartwheels.
I mean, it's like being in a zoo.

Playgrounds are such sporty places
Know what I mean?
Everyone seems to kick a ball,
Race each other and throw objects.
I mean, it's like being in the Olympic Games.

Playgrounds are such crazy places,
Know what I mean?
Everyone seems to jump, do handstands,
Cartwheels and do crazy dances.
I mean, it's like being in a circus.

Amy Pickard (9)
St Mark's Elm Tree Primary School, Fairfield

The Swamp

The swamp is scary,
The werewolf's very hairy,
In the graveyard there are creatures,
They have disgusting features,
The armour doesn't seem to move,
The bats and vampires are having a groove,
The Grim Reaper's reaping,
The skeletons are sleeping,
The mummies in their coffins,
Making bad pizza toppings,
I'm staring death in the face,
I'm getting out of this haunted place.

Jack Rutter (10)
St Mark's Elm Tree Primary School, Fairfield

Playgrounds

Playgrounds are such cheerful places,
Know what I mean?
Everyone seems to
Laugh, play, smile and sing.
I mean it's like being in a funfair.

Playgrounds are such brainy places,
Know what I mean?
Everyone seems to be
Mathematicians, scientists and just plain clever.
I mean it's like being in an exam room.

Playgrounds are such bossy places.
Know what I mean?
Everyone seems to say, 'You're not allowed that, go away
And those shoes are illegal.'
Everyone except me because I'm kind.

Beth Cash (9)
St Mark's Elm Tree Primary School, Fairfield

Questions

Do sharks get tired of eating fish?
Do squirrels get tired of climbing trees?
Do hedgehogs get tired of having spiky fur?
Do hens get tired of laying eggs?

Are pigs bored of squealing?
Are birds bored of flying?
Are bears bored of being scary?
Are tigers bored of roaring?

Do dogs tire of barking?
Do cats tire of scratching?
Do bees tire of collecting honey?
This pen tires of writing!

Megan Bullas (9)
St Mark's Elm Tree Primary School, Fairfield

Playgrounds

Playgrounds are such creative places,
Know what I mean?
Everyone seems to have something to sketch, draw and make,
I mean, it's like being in an art gallery.

Playgrounds are such crazy places,
Know what I mean?
Everyone has something to cheer, roar and scream about,
I mean, it's like being in a jungle.

Playgrounds are such colourful places,
Know what I mean?
Everyone has something to sing, design and giggle about,
I mean, it's like being in a rainbow.

But most importantly everyone has something to talk about,
I mean, everyone has to whisper, chit-chat and talk,
I mean, it's like being in a monkey show.
(But with all the noise it's still a great playground.)

Jade Taylor (9)
St Mark's Elm Tree Primary School, Fairfield

Untitled

Do books get tired of being read?
Do dogs get tired of walking?
Are computers tired of working?
Are books tired of being written in?
Do toys get tired of being played with?
Do bumblebees tire of bumbling?
Are butterflies tired of flowers?
Are babies tired of crawling?
I don't know all the answers
But I'll ask them all one day.
I get tired of working
But never tired of play.

Sophie Clarkson (9)
St Mark's Elm Tree Primary School, Fairfield

Playgrounds

Playgrounds are such fun places
Know what I mean?
Everyone seems to
Run, jump, talk and do cartwheels.
I mean, it's like being in a zoo.

Playgrounds are such sporty places
Know what I mean?
Everyone seems to
Kick a ball, race each other and throw objects.
I mean, it's like being in the Olympic games.

Playgrounds are such wacky places
Know what I mean?
Everyone seems to
Dance like a maniac, run and shout.
I mean, it's like being in a horror movie.

Laura Hood (9)
St Mark's Elm Tree Primary School, Fairfield

Trees Are Great

Trees are great
I saw one on its date
Dancing around and drinking
Holding hands
Singing and grooving.

So answer me please
If there weren't any trees
Where would we get our beds to sleep?
Where would squirrels get their nuts?
Where would we get chairs to sit on?
Where would we get our fruit from?

Joshua Phipps (7)
St Mark's Elm Tree Primary School, Fairfield

Questions

Do chairs get tired of being sat on?
Do monkeys get tired of swinging?
Does chewing gum get tired of being chewed?
Do people get tired of walking?

Are flowers tired of growing?
Are cars tired of moving?
Are clocks tired of ticking?
Do birds get tired of flying?

Do trays get tired of getting pushed and pulled?
Do books get tired of opening and closing?
Do computers get tired of typing?
Do stars get tired of twinkling?

I do not know the answers
I'll ask them all one day
But I'll get tired of working
But never tired of play.

Paige Young (9)
St Mark's Elm Tree Primary School, Fairfield

Trees Are Great

Trees are great, they love to skate
They always stand and wait
To estimate how many leaves altogether are
On their branches.

So answer me please
If there weren't any trees
Where would we get paper from?
Where would squirrels get their nuts from?
Where would we build our hideouts?
Where would owls sleep?

Abbie Stoddart (8)
St Mark's Elm Tree Primary School, Fairfield

Playgrounds

Playgrounds are such hurtful places
Know what I mean?
Everyone seems to have to
Be thrown about, pushed, squashed and pulled about
I mean, it's like being on a motorway.

Playgrounds are such noisy places
Know what I mean?
Everyone seems to
Have something to moan about, groan, cry and argue about
I mean, it's like being in a debate.

Playgrounds are such friendly places
Know what I mean?
Everyone seems to
Make up clubs, games teams and passwords
Everyone *including me*
Know what I mean?

Rebecca Alexander & Emily Robinson (9)
St Mark's Elm Tree Primary School, Fairfield

Trees Are Great

Trees are great
Their mothers do not smack them when they have been naughty
They don't need excuses
Or go to school and learn their two times tables.

So answer me please
If there weren't any trees
Where would owls sleep?
How would people run about?
Where would squirrels live?
Where would we get wooden chairs?

Emma Armstrong (7)
St Mark's Elm Tree Primary School, Fairfield

Playgrounds

Playgrounds are such rushy places.
Know what I mean?
Everyone seems to have something to talk about,
Shout about and laugh about.
I mean, it's like being in a year two classroom!

Playgrounds are such noisy places.
Know what I mean?
Everyone seems to have something to argue about,
Rush about and shove about.
I mean, it's like World War Two.

Playgrounds are such unfriendly places.
Know what I mean?
Everyone seems to have something to moan
And groan and whisper about.
I mean, it's like jail.

Harry Teasdale (9)
St Mark's Elm Tree Primary School, Fairfield

Questions

Do dogs get tired of barking?
Do cats get bored with miaowing?
Do birds get tired of singing?
Do sheep get bored with baa-ing?

Do bees get tired of flying?
Do ladybirds get bored with sleeping?
Do rabbits get tired of bouncing?
Do monkeys get tired of eating bananas?

Do lions get tired of roaring?
Do horses get bored with galloping?
Do pigs get tired of oinking?
Do dolphins get tired of swimming?

I don't know any of these
But I know that I love working.

Abbie Wilkinson (9)
St Mark's Elm Tree Primary School, Fairfield

Playgrounds

Playgrounds are such magical places
Know what I mean?
Everyone seems to
Spin around, twist and run about
I mean, it's like a merry-go-round.

Playgrounds are such muddy places
Know what I mean?
Everyone seems to
Jump in muddy puddles and splash each other
I mean, it's just like a swamp.

Playgrounds are such peaceful places
Know what I mean?
Everyone seems to whisper, play quiet games
And they don't shout at each other.
I mean, it's like being in a library every day.

Alun Littlefair (9)
St Mark's Elm Tree Primary School, Fairfield

The Grim Reaper

I'm being chased by the Grim Reaper,
As I'm running, I'm getting weaker!

I'm being chased by the Grim Reaper,
I'm jumping over the jeeper's creeper!

I'm being chased by the Grim Reaper,
My legs are getting cheaper!

I'm being chased by the Grim Reaper,
I'm walking across a sleeper!

I'm being chased by the Grim Reaper,
The chasm's getting deeper!

I'm being chased by the Grim Reaper,
He's got me!

Nicholas Williams (9)
St Mark's Elm Tree Primary School, Fairfield

Trees Are Great

Trees are great
They like to estimate with their mates
How many leaves are on their plates.

So answer me please
If there weren't any trees
Where would bees hang their honey?
Where would squirrels hide?
Where would we make our dens?
Where would birds tweet and sing?

Lucas Connor (7)
St Mark's Elm Tree Primary School, Fairfield

Dogs

Dogs are always happy,
They never get worn out,
Always ready to play.

Always wanting food,
Never annoying or silly,
Always cute and cuddly
And are man's best friend.

Oliver Riddle (9)
St Mark's Elm Tree Primary School, Fairfield

Elephant

Huge, fat and giant,
Big, moving mountain,
Dull and grey, loud and noisy,
Flappy ears, pointed tusks,
Heavy as a sumo wrestler.

Mark Hill (9)
St Mark's Elm Tree Primary School, Fairfield

Dragons

A dragon is a fierce animal,
Fierce like I say.

They fly around burning things,
Every single day.

Dragons are scary,
Very scary indeed.

They fly and fly and fly,
'Til it's time to feed.

Kirsty Harrison (10)
St Mark's Elm Tree Primary School, Fairfield

Memory

Pig fat candles for light,
Just not at night.
Quiet as a mouse
Which runs through the house.
Up the stairs to bed,
As they lay their head.

The seagulls squawking,
As we're walking.
Fresh, green grass,
As shiny as brass.

At the priory,
We have to write in our diary.
We got close to the well,
And nearly fell.
We all had fun,
In the sun.

Alexandra Topliffe (10)
Teesside Preparatory & High School, Eaglescliffe

Memories

We are walking to the priory on a cold, windy day
We look at the old ruins crumbling away
The grand pillars holding up the walls
The rainbow arch looking very tall.

I saw the place where the monks would pray
I went to their beds where they would lay
All the walls with rotting stones
And through it all the wind moans.

We walked out of the priory with information in my head
'You've done very well today,' my teacher said
I will remember this priory with its statues
I would recommend this place to you.

Mona Ansari Beni (10)
Teesside Preparatory & High School, Eaglescliffe

Memory

The priory was so very old
And the wind was really cold,
The rainbow arch was so tall
Making a door in the rotting wall.

The pillars holding the roof of the aisles
Nothing like this for miles
I heard the priest in my head
But I knew he'd long been dead.

I saw the remains of a well
Full of secrets nobody could tell
I saw the place where the monks would pray
I will always remember that brilliant day.

Lucy Atha (10)
Teesside Preparatory & High School, Eaglescliffe

Memory

I sat on the grass,
Took a deep breath,
Closed my eyes,
Silent as death.

I hear my pencil
And open my eyes,
See dazzling seagulls,
Inside, my favourite pictures circling in my head,
Glide and swoop, over them I mull.

I see sitting in front of me,
A large, shadowy tower, no more,
Full of magic in the air,
One old, creaking, shivery, fantasy of a door.

　　My memory!

Kathryn Rose Howard (10)
Teesside Preparatory & High School, Eaglescliffe

Memory

I heard the wind blowing through the trees,
I heard the birds singing in the breeze.
I heard the sea rushing onto the shore,
As we walked slowly towards the priory door.

I look at the arch all battered and worn,
Over years gone by it got more torn.
We walked on past the priory door,
As we stepped down onto the deep moss floor.

I will always remember,
The day we went.
It had such a special scent.

Jenny Costello (10)
Teesside Preparatory & High School, Eaglescliffe

Memory

The ruins were cold and lonely,
The arch hung like a bird in the sky,
The grass was wet with dew.

The gulls squawked in the distance on the sea,
The wind, icy and roaring.
The stones were patterned like scrolled writing.

I felt cold and tired in the neglected air,
We were sat in silence looking at the priory ruins.

Annie Rennison (10)
Teesside Preparatory & High School, Eaglescliffe

Memory

I was there, was it true, was it?
I could hear birds, beautiful birds,
Ships rocking in the evening dock,
The sea waves clashing against the headland.

I was with my friends in silence,
My tummy rumbled, I was cold,
Strangely excited I felt,
Everything around me was cold.

Charlotte Jarred (10)
Teesside Preparatory & High School, Eaglescliffe

Memory

Cold coming at me like a sharp knife.
The wind whizzing and whirling, angrily, full of life.
Listening to silence, that's what I could hear.
The trees swooping gracefully, watching them as they come near.
The sun almost set, the grass very wet.
We made our way home but little did we care,
For it's in our memories and will always be there.

Grace Sherratt (10)
Teesside Preparatory & High School, Eaglescliffe

Memory

There I sat as cold as ice,
Whilst the wind blew around me.
Looking up at the rainbow arch,
At Lindisfarne Priory.

The sea in the distance,
The birds in the trees,
The sheep in the field,
And there sat me.

The rainbow arch was tall and clear,
Towering over me like an ancient tree.
The bricks, jagged, brown and white,
Damp and old, and extremely cold.

The silence was all around,
Listening to itself.
Sitting there on the floor,
I make a memory.

Joanne Sayer (10)
Teesside Preparatory & High School, Eaglescliffe

Memory

I have a little memory,
Of a priory ever so old,
Most of it in ruins,
The stones patterned, but cold.

I have a little memory,
Where I can hear the sheep across the wall,
The night was a magnificent colour,
Because the sun was just about to fall.

I have a little memory,
It is as old as old can be,
But I know,
That it will stay a memory for me.

Jessica Hope Lister (10)
Teesside Preparatory & High School, Eaglescliffe

Memory

I could feel the cool breeze as it prickled my skin,
I could smell fresh dew, moisture so cold,
A magical world, its ruins so eerie,
The story of time starts to unfold.

Hear the sea, swishing softly against the jetty,
See the sunset pink, yellow, scarlet and amber,
Casting dark shadows below the arches,
Hear the chatter of birds perched on a tower.

I can feel autumn memories shining ever stronger,
Feel the peace of people who came to rest,
The love of the ruins, looked after so well,
I will live and this memory I shall tell.

Emily Frances Willis (11)
Teesside Preparatory & High School, Eaglescliffe

Memory

I sit upon the dewy grass,
Seeing an old, broken tower,
The mist clinging on like a child,
An old arch creaking in the wind.

The sun runs behind a large cloud,
The small walls mark the simple rooms,
The wind turns down its loud volume,
Everything quiet as a grave.

I feel my ears growing icicles,
I pull my coat closer round me,
The wind wraps itself closer to me,
We wander out of this ancient place.

Victoria Peacock (11)
Teesside Preparatory & High School, Eaglescliffe

Memories

Lindisfarne Priory stands alone,
Away from the mainland, all on its own,
Built by the monks centuries past,
Made from stone and to last.

The ruins look so drab and dull,
Years ago, they used to be full.
Monks doing their daily chores
Trying to remember all of God's laws.

I walked around the cold, rocky place,
With the wind blowing in my face.
The rainbow arch stood in front of me,
The carvings so beautiful for all to see.

Sadly it's just a ruin now,
And to the wind it has to bow.
I enjoyed my visit and hope and pray,
That it manages to stand another day.

Joni McDonough (10)
Teesside Preparatory & High School, Eaglescliffe

Memory

Memory of the priory,
Tapping feet along the stone floor,
Someone was writing a diary,
They weren't allowed to talk.

I saw the fire, big, strong and bolted.
I kept on walking down the nave,
I saw the stairs battered, gone and mouldered,
It felt like I was old.

I will always remember this time,
I really don't know how,
Maybe I will think of lime,
Then it will return to my mind.

Lucy Smith (10)
Teesside Preparatory & High School, Eaglescliffe

Memory

It was a cold, dark and gusty day,
The hour we went to see the monks pray.
The wind was blowing right through my face,
I walked hurriedly just in case.

The monks prayed with great devotions,
Scared I was to make commotion.
They prayed and prayed till half-past eight,
For us that sounds a bit too late.

There it still stands, the visit to the priory,
And it takes up 7 pages in my diary.
When I grow up I'm sure to go back.
Maybe I'll have something more to crack!

Vidya Shyam Sundar (11)
Teesside Preparatory & High School, Eaglescliffe

Memories

It was a cold and cool evening,
In the priory watching monks sing.
With my friends talking around me,
Watching everything I could see.

I heard the boats rocking on the sea,
As I felt my body fill with glee.
The cold wind was blowing from the sea,
It really gave great delight to me.

I will remember the priory,
By making a special memory.
This memory shall be about me,
When I went to the old priory.

Laura Awad (10)
Teesside Preparatory & High School, Eaglescliffe

Memory

On the cold, dark, windy day
We were inside the priory
The priory was all broken down
But I can feel the old priory.

I can hear the sea splashing
The boat coming into the shore
The birds gathering on the priory
On top of the beautiful arch.

I close my eyes and imagine
That I am floating in the past
When the monks sing beautifully
And pray in peaceful silence.

When I become an adult
I'll never forget these memories
These beautiful, wonderful memories
Remain with me forever.

Nicole Wang (10)
Teesside Preparatory & High School, Eaglescliffe

Memory

About the priory, old books and stones,
I saw such a sight,
A dark day to step inside
When I got in I felt so warm
To feel all the excitement and what the monks wore.
We were jotting and stuffing our books with knowledge
That was for school.
I was thrilled to see the rainbow arch.
This was an outstanding memory for me.

Kate Bradley (11)
Teesside Preparatory & High School, Eaglescliffe

Memory

Once up on a time,
I was watching the shadows,
As the sun melted away,
Behind the priory's arch.
The grass was as soft as cotton wool.
I remembered my home,
My bedroom so cool.

I could hear the wind,
Talking to me gently.
The birds were chattering,
And praising themselves.
I remember the beach,
With not a single sound.
Lovely and beautiful.

What did I smell?
Nothing but sea air.
I imagined and thought,
This is a wonderful rhyme,
And shall end as it started,
Once upon a time!

Sanaya Dhir (10)
Teesside Preparatory & High School, Eaglescliffe

Memories

I could hear the sea so far from me.
The island so small, that tower so tall.
The priory so near it's like it was never here.

As I look at the priory door it's such a glore.
I can feel the wind blowing at my face
It really is a cold place.

Eve Bannatyne (11)
Teesside Preparatory & High School, Eaglescliffe

Memory

I sat in the grass
My pencil in hand,
Wind in my face,
Watching the sand.

Lonely and peaceful,
Is what I felt,
Looking at the brick
Arrows, curves and welts.

The cold breeze
Whipping the sea,
A bell in my ear
A memory for me.

Laura Jayne Hall (10)
Teesside Preparatory & High School, Eaglescliffe

Memory

I saw no windows,
I saw bricks that were cubes,
A well that was circular,
I felt some strange happiness.

I could hear seagulls
Or could it be the bells?
The priory came alive,
As I waved the sun goodbye.

The moon was going up,
As we were going down,
I turned around,
Goodbye, but I'll remember.

Georgina Keel (10)
Teesside Preparatory & High School, Eaglescliffe

Memory

The priory old and darkness full,
The wind blowing a lonely seagull.

Bleak yet peaceful at the priory
We stepped off, the world we could see.

The memories we made will be in our heads to stay,
I'll go to bed and dream the things I've done this day.

Fiona Wingrove (10)
Teesside Preparatory & High School, Eaglescliffe

How Does A Rabbit Move?

How does a rabbit move?
As slow as a tortoise,
As fast as a cheetah.
How does a rabbit move?

What does a rabbit look like?
As beautiful as a butterfly,
As ugly as a spider.
What does a rabbit look like?

Where does a rabbit live?
In a hole so small,
In a house so big.
Where does a rabbit live?

What's a rabbit's best friend?
A human so friendly,
A deer so shy.
What's a rabbit's best friend?

Elizabeth Hall (8)
William Cassidi CE Primary School, Stillington

Food, The Terrible Truth!

Take some carrots, take some peas,
Sprawling with flies and fleas,
Get some bread, nice and thick,
Be sure it won't make you sick.
Have some pasta, just one meal,
It might be a slippery eel!
Try some salad, one whole dish,
It could taste of rotten fish.
Careful when you eat your food,
The food you eat could be crude!
Taste the tuna, it is great,
Will you suffer the fishy fate?
Lick your lips at fruit and veg,
It tastes of your neighbour's hedge.
Lovely pastries and crisp cake,
See the bugs and the noise they make.
Biscuits are nice, yoghurt's good,
Thick and creamy, full of mud.
Careful when you eat your food,
The food you eat could be *crude!*

Kate Newman (10)
William Cassidi CE Primary School, Stillington

Happiness

Happiness is when you are
Being filled with joy,
Happiness is Christmas
When you get presents,
Happiness is Boxing Day
When cousins come around,
Happiness is love
We love our mums.

Christopher Ranby (7)
William Cassidi CE Primary School, Stillington

My Cute Little Bunny

I have a bunny,
Who is as cute as a teddy.
So I decided,
To call it Eddy!

It has long fluffy ears,
It doesn't have any fears.
It has a tiny precious tail,
It can sprint further than a snail!

I love my little bunny,
Who is as cute as a teddy.
Who is also called Eddy.

Rebecca Alderson (8)
William Cassidi CE Primary School, Stillington

What Does A Panda Do?

What does a panda do?
Does it sit around sleeping
Or eat bamboo?

What does a panda move like?
As slow as a tortoise
Or as fast as a bike?

Where does a panda live?
In the deep, dark jungle
Or in the city so big?

I don't know, do you?

Samantha Catchpole (8)
William Cassidi CE Primary School, Stillington

A Beautiful . . .

Food nicker,
Sleepy head,
Fur ball,
Cuddly,
Fast,
Funny,
Fun,
Crazy,
Mad,
Bouncy,
Male,
Fluffy and
Bone chaser.
It's a . . .
Dog!

Stephanie Barnett (8)
William Cassidi CE Primary School, Stillington

Computers

Computers big,
Computers small,
Computers short,
Computers tall,
Computers fat,
Computers thin,
Speakers,
That make a din,
Made of plasma, plastic, glass
You can't just throw it in the trash.

Kirsten Barnett (11)
William Cassidi CE Primary School, Stillington

It's A . . .

Colour-changer,
Slow-mover,
Multi-colour,
Tree-changer,
Sun-catcher,
Rain-chaser,
Rainbow-catcher,
High-lighter.
It's a colour changing
Chameleon.

Josh Moody (8)
William Cassidi CE Primary School, Stillington

Dog

Cat hunter
Loud barker
Noisy chewer
Quick runner
Loud sleeper
Zzzzzzz.
Guess what it is . . .
A dog!

Ellie Alexander (8)
William Cassidi CE Primary School, Stillington

Cats

Cats, cats, cats are fun,
Cats, cats, cats for everyone,
Cats are here, cats are there,
Cats are nearly everywhere!

Jessica Dixon (8)
William Cassidi CE Primary School, Stillington

Butterflies

B utterflies are beautiful
U sually colourful
T ell your mum you have seen a butterfly
T oday people they are kind
E veryone likes them
R ound and round they go
F or everyone
L ovely for you
Y ou like them, don't you?

Shannon Harbron (8)
William Cassidi CE Primary School, Stillington

Homework

H omework is easy,
O nly when you know it,
M y mum sometimes helps me,
E mily, my sister, helps me a bit,
W hen we get tricky homework it's hard to understand,
O ranges help me work,
R ebecca, my friend, never helps me,
K ind of tricky some nights!

Sophie Burton (8)
William Cassidi CE Primary School, Stillington

Frogs

F is for fitness what frogs do best,
R is for resting on a lily pad nice and cool,
O is for oxygen for frogs to live,
G is for green that makes frogs cool,
S is for swimming in a cool, cold pond.

Haris Shamoon (8)
William Cassidi CE Primary School, Stillington

Butterfly

B is for beautiful,
U is for unusual,
T is for turquoise on its wings,
T is for twinkling,
E is for exotic,
R is for red,
F is for flowers that they love,
L is for leaves that they sit on,
Y is for yellow spots,

Butterflies are beautiful!

Marina-Josephina Gears (7)
William Cassidi CE Primary School, Stillington

Animals

A nts, small and friendly.
N ewts, slimy and rare.
I ce dogs, furry and fast.
M ammals, warm-blooded creatures.
A ttic is home to spiders and rats.
L ettuce is a bunny's best food.
S piders, vicious and hairy.

John Titchener (7)
William Cassidi CE Primary School, Stillington

Trees

T rees dropping leaves like planes dropping bombs.
R ain falls to make them grow.
E ven when it doesn't rain it is still very vain.
E veryone cuts them down but stop them we will.
S trong it will be.

Adam James Glass (9)
William Cassidi CE Primary School, Stillington

Monsters In My Cupboard

I can hear breathing in my cupboard
I can hear a knock at the door
I can hear tapping at the window
I think those were monsters
I know they were
Goodnight
Don't let the monsters bite!

Christopher Taylor (7)
William Cassidi CE Primary School, Stillington

Happiness

Happiness is when you eat chocolate,
Happiness is gymnastics,
Happiness is when you play outside,
Happiness is when you get to watch a funny film,
Happiness is when you stay up late,
Happiness is a way of life.

Thomas Liam Holdsworth (7)
William Cassidi CE Primary School, Stillington

Disappointment

Disappointment is when you are freezing.
Disappointment is when your best friend is on holiday.

Disappointment is when you have to get up
But it's not school.
Disappointment is a way of life.

Daniel Butler (7)
William Cassidi CE Primary School, Stillington

Henry VIII

Henry VIII, I was his biggest fan,
Even though he was a very fat man.
Old Henry's life was rough,
Just as well because he was tough.
He had loads of wives,
And loads of knives,
Because when he married them
A few days later he carried them.

Eliot Barley (9)
William Cassidi CE Primary School, Stillington

The Great Fire Of London

It all started off in Pudding Lane in a baker's shop.
The fire blazed through the glass as the red monster grew,
Burning the wood it escaped through the building
And spread to the next.
Two hours passed and London was burnt.
The black ashes dead.

Adam Wells (9)
William Cassidi CE Primary School, Stillington

Autumn Leaves

Autumn leaves are falling off trees.
Plants and flowers are dying
And they are trying and trying
To keep alive but some of them
Are not surviving.

Chloe Bloomfield (9)
William Cassidi CE Primary School, Stillington

It's A . . .?

It lives in water.
Sucks blood.
Moves slow.
Is so small
And it's black.
You can hardly see it
In the water.
It's a bit slimy.
It's a . . .
Leech.

Ioannis Daniel Kolios (8)
William Cassidi CE Primary School, Stillington

Happiness

Happiness is playing out,
Happiness is healthy eating,
Happiness is loving my family,
Happiness is playing golf,
Happiness is playing football,
Happiness is school.

Liam Osborne (8)
William Cassidi CE Primary School, Stillington

Happiness

Happiness is having a nice quiet night,
Happiness is having the sun shining on my back on holiday,
Happiness is playing with the dogs,
Happiness is waking up on Christmas Day,
Happiness is my way of life.

Nicholas Abrahams (7)
William Cassidi CE Primary School, Stillington

Colours

I don't like cabbage
I don't like peas
I don't like broccoli
Or anything green.

I don't like peppers
I don't like sauce
I don't like eating anything
That's red of course.

But the food I like
I'm sure you can guess
I eat chocolate so fast
My face is a mess.

Gayle Tait (10)
William Cassidi CE Primary School, Stillington

Gorillas

Gorillas are giants,
Gorillas swing in the jungle,
Gorillas are strong,
Gorillas growl in the jungle,
Gorillas thump their chests.

Andrew Hawes (7)
William Cassidi CE Primary School, Stillington

My . . . Dog

Barking all the time.
Playing and following me everywhere.
Everywhere he is there wagging his tail at me.
Eating everything up.

Fleur Durham (8)
William Cassidi CE Primary School, Stillington

Flowers

F lowers are such pretty things,
L iking the sunshine, loving the rain,
O range, yellow, red flowers,
W aiting for water to drink,
E very flower is a different shape,
R oses are red and smell so nice,
S hining at everyone every day.

Flowers are everywhere I look!

Grace Maloney (7)
William Cassidi CE Primary School, Stillington

Mum And Dad

M um is cuddly,
U nusual she is,
M um does the ironing and washing.

And

D ad is fun,
A nd he drives fast,
D ad makes lovely food.

William King (7)
William Cassidi CE Primary School, Stillington

Lions

L ying down sleeping,
I n a second leaping,
O n me!
N ever disturb a lion,
S o don't stay up late or he will eat you!

Oliver Bell (7)
William Cassidi CE Primary School, Stillington

Playground

P laygrounds are the best place to play.
L ots of things to do each day.
A game of tig or maybe skipping.
Y our watch is fast but time is ticking.
G reat games, jumping and throwing.
R unning games, dashing and darting.
O utside with our friends is fun.
U nder trees we talk and chatter.
N ever do the games get boring.
D on't rain today!

Alexandra Cornelius (9)
William Cassidi CE Primary School, Stillington

School

S ucceed in school.
C ome on, do more work.
H elp people who are stuck.
O h school is good, isn't it?
O K, lunchtime everyone.
L earn your times tables.

Eleanor Smith (9)
William Cassidi CE Primary School, Stillington

Memories

I really don't know,
Why I'm leaving memories in the snow.
Where I grew up when I was small,
Where I left my monster in the hall.
Where I kept my little pet mouse,
I really don't want to leave my house.

Holly Armstrong (10)
William Cassidi CE Primary School, Stillington

Autumn

Crunching, munching,
Children playing with leaves upon the ground.
Darker nights drawing near,
As I wait with no fear.
When I walk on the crunchy leaves,
I hear an owl hoot.
As I walk through Oak Hill Park
It starts to rain because it's . . .
    Autumn.

Rebecca Drew (10)
William Cassidi CE Primary School, Stillington

My Best Friend Kate

We play on the swings all day, all night,
We sleep at each other's houses every Friday night.
We play together all the time,
She makes me laugh, we're both very daft.
We talk about the friends we've got,
She always says you're my best friend,
And I reply you will always be my best friend!

Alice Constantine (10)
William Cassidi CE Primary School, Stillington

Big Ben

Big Ben standing tall,
Watching you go past,
Chiming on the hour like a massive tower.
Very, very tall, the clock is like a ball.
A hen is like a ball.
A hen is very small
But Big Ben is very tall.

Ben Wells (9)
William Cassidi CE Primary School, Stillington

My Hamster Kennings

Mini-walker
Non-talker
Tiny-stroller
Wheel-roller
Blood-drawer
Wire-gnawer
Wool-ripper
Water-sipper
Day-sleeper
Night-creeper.

Lewis Cotts (9)
William Cassidi CE Primary School, Stillington

Jupiter

Jupiter, the king of space,
The biggest planet in our universe,
A gas giant.
Its great, red spot terrifying all who have seen it.
If one was to get near to it
They would be sucked in by its powerful force.
Volcanoes erupt on the surface every hour.

Mathew Robinson (9)
William Cassidi CE Primary School, Stillington

My Best Friend Alice

Me and Alice play on the swings all day.
My mum says she is not real.
But she is, she lives in my cupboard.
She has a tiger, elephant and parrot as pets,
Alice is gone now,
I'm too old for an imaginary friend.

Kate Wilkinson (9)
William Cassidi CE Primary School, Stillington

Magic Garden

I found the key
To that gold-painted door
I couldn't wait anymore.

I put in the key
I unlocked the door
I couldn't stop for tea.

I took my time to go inside
There was magic before my eyes!
My thoughts went wild in my mind.

There were trees with fruit of all kinds
Flowers of every colour
I heard foxes rustling, birds sing and laughter of children.

Rachael Ross (9)
William Cassidi CE Primary School, Stillington

A Hole In One

The course lies ahead of me.
I stand at the first tee.

I swing my club and hit the ball.
In the distance I see it fall.

Is it possible? What have I done?
Yes! I've got a hole in one!

Paul Ruddle (9)
William Cassidi CE Primary School, Stillington

Rainforest

Toucans pecking fruit with their beaks,
Water dripping on the many leaves,
Monkeys swinging through the rain,
The sun is a stranger as it shines through the trees.

Isaac Allen (7)
William Cassidi CE Primary School, Stillington

The Weather And The Seasons

It is winter,
Everyone is indoors.
Curtains are closed,
Fires are roaring,
Snowmen are made.

Spring is here,
Baby lambs appear.
Daffodils are opening,
They're as golden as the sun.

Summer is here,
The sun is shining.
The birds and people are relaxing,
In the sun.

Now it is autumn,
The leaves have changed colour.
They have become crisp.
Raindrops are patting
And pouncing on the road.
It stops.
The sun is shining
And a rainbow is shining.

Hannah Norman (9)
William Cassidi CE Primary School, Stillington

Lively Flowers

You can see the bright flowers from far away,
The flowers smell so nice.
Colourful flowers are so bright,
Flowers are so pretty and beautiful.
The flowers blow when it's windy,
Flowers are cheerful.
The flowers are lively,
They are so lovely.

Olivia Durham (9)
William Cassidi CE Primary School, Stillington

Don't Be So Rude

You should not be rude,
While you eat your food,
One thing you must not do,
Is speak while you chew,
What will other people think,
If you slurp when you drink?

When old people are standing on the bus,
Give up your seat without a fuss,
If you get caught in the rain,
Do not use the Lord's name in vain,
Because no one wants to hear you swear,
Just because you have wet hair.

So remember, don't be bad,
Be polite and you will be glad,
When people think how nice you are,
With good manners you'll go far.

Dale Howe (9)
William Cassidi CE Primary School, Stillington

Smashing Sports

Speedo goggles, down the lane,
No swimmer is in pain.

Cracking cricket, he hits the ball,
Whacks it completely over the wall.

Flipping football, fouls all around,
Lots of players on the ground.

Troublesome trampolining, there's no stopping them,
Come on, come on, the Englishmen!

Christopher Michael Holdsworth (9)
William Cassidi CE Primary School, Stillington

Rugby

Sunday morning it's rugby day
I've trained so hard I hope I play
I'll run, push and tackle all day
If coach picks me for the team today.

The team is picked and I am chosen
It's wintertime and the pitch is frozen
The whistle blows and the game begins
I get the ball and pass to the wing.

The ball comes back and I am tackled
Over the line I fly and score a try
I hear the crowd shout and cry
The whistle blows, our team have won.

The county cup is within our grasp
And we'll be the champions at last.

Elliot Sharp (9)
William Cassidi CE Primary School, Stillington

Rough Rugby

I place the ball on the cone,
I got the penalty from a foul throw.
The opponent kicked me and it hurt real bad,
But I didn't cry like a wimpy lad.
My sport is rugby, I'm on a team,
We're brilliant, what a dream.
Last week our team badly lost,
Probably because I was off.
The other day we beat a team,
I was so hot my blood was steam.
We do team practice on a Friday,
We play matches on a Sunday.
In a few weeks we're having a rugby fun day.

Chris Holmes (9)
William Cassidi CE Primary School, Stillington

Spring

Winter has gone,
And I am one.

Springtime

Grass is green,
No one is mean.

Springtime

New animals are born,
As I play the French horn.

Springtime

Children laughing happily,
As their hearts beat rapidly.

Springtime's a wonderful thing.

Helen French (9)
William Cassidi CE Primary School, Stillington

Football

Football's dangerous, football's mad
Football is very bad.

Football's mean,
Yes it is, you'll have to be very lean.

Eat healthy food,
Don't you dare get in a mood.

Listen to the crowd,
They're very loud.

Go and score,
Maybe even more.

Luke Johnson (9)
William Cassidi CE Primary School, Stillington

My Home

(Inspired by 'Magic Box' by Kit Wright)

I will put in my home . . .
A midsummer sunset,
A tip of a tree,
And an autumn walk for you and me.

I will put in my home . . .
A leaf of knowledge
A diamond of joy,
And a book for every girl and boy.

I will put in my home . . .
The wavy sea
And a rainbow of peace
A warm and cosy fleece.

My home is made from . . .
Satin silk
Plaited gold
With not a speck of mould.
I shall swim in a pool of jewels in my home.

Olivia McLurg (9)
Yarm CP School, Yarm

Titanic

Titanic was the greatest ship
It was the queen of the sea
Triple class used by everyone
After sailing, sinking prevailed
Never has a bigger disaster been reported
It never made it to its destination
'cause it sank.
Goodbye Titanic.

Anand Krishna (8)
Yarm CP School, Yarm

The Magic House

(Inspired by 'Magic Box' by Kit Wright)

I will put in my house . . .
The smell of lavender to settle you to sleep.
The smell of a spray of perfume to make you sniff it in.

I will put in my house . . .
A bed of pink and purple flowers.
A magic carpet to float you to every stop.
A room to store my secrets in.
A tree full of small birds.

I will put in my house . . .
My happy family to bring love and jollity to my perfect life.
My pony and our pets to keep me company.
My family portrait to remember my family forever and ever.
My bed to keep me relaxed and comfortable.
My house is made from bricks, flowers and precious stones.
I will dance in my house and be jolly forever and ever.

Kate Chapman (9)
Yarm CP School, Yarm

Titanic

Feeling frantic, panic in the air.
As the ship hits the deadly iceberg.
Freezing cold water splashing the deck,
Screaming passengers,
Sorrowful faces as the ship tilts steeper.
Nothing is happy,
Everyone is getting onto lifeboats,
Bangs as distress rockets are fired.
The boat splits in two
Then a huge splash as the Titanic plunges down deep . . .

Matthew Harkin (8)
Yarm CP School, Yarm

The Imaginative House

(Inspired by 'Magic Box' by Kit Wright)

I will put in my home . . .
A jungle of ten white tigers,
Sleeping and stalking for animals of prey to survive their jungle lives,
They're just as rare as golden treasure.

I will put in my home . . .
A rainforest of parrots and macaws
Swooping and sawing through the air
And singing in their nests slowly and calmly,
They're just as lovely as Christmas Day.

I will put in my home . . .
Three fast cheetahs fierce and wealthy
In the colour of peanut and honey,
Sleeping in layers of leaves,
Doing nearly nothing but snoring and dreaming.

Chloe Caygill (9)
Yarm CP School, Yarm

The Queen Of The Sea

Titanic was the queen of the sea
She set sail at Southampton
She sailed over the Atlantic Ocean
Titanic was very big, bigger than the Two Towers upwards.
She crashed into an iceberg
She got brought down
Woman and children first
Women and children got in the lifeboats
Hoping to be found
Gladly Carpathia came to help
We saved seven hundred and five passengers
That was the end of the legendary Titanic.

Holly Conroy (8)
Yarm CP School, Yarm

The House

(Inspired by 'Magic Box' by Kit Wright)

I will put in my house . . .
A feather for goodwill to the people in it,
A parrot bringing colour to the home,
A pack of dogs bringing happiness to the home.

I will put in my home . . .
A trampoline bouncing you up to Heaven,
A clown to cheer you up when you're upset,
A studio so you can show people how you feel.

I will put in my house . . .
My best friend to be there for me all the time,
A long grassed garden full of hollyhocks
To know you always have a friend there,
A rainbow full of magical dreams to come true.

I will put in my house . . .
The moon in the attic so it's a magical thought,
A stable to keep horses in so you can ride them when you're bored,
A roller coaster so when you're feeling down
And have a frown you'll soon be happy,
'Cause you're in the air looking down at the ground.

Alexandra King (9)
Yarm CP School, Yarm

The Voyage Of The Titanic

A long time ago, when fireworks were setting,
The Titanic set sail.
Everyone cheered as she left the dock.
A couple of days later disaster happened,
The ship hit an iceberg.
Water rushed in,
As one end started to sink people were screaming for help
That was the legend of the Titanic.

Beth Myers (8)
Yarm CP School, Yarm

Titanic Disaster

Titanic was the biggest ship
Heading for New York
In the misty seas of the Atlantic panic struck
Women, children abandoned to lifeboats
Into the icy graves they drifted
Carpathia came to the rescue
But only some survived
Titanic, it sunk.

Kevin Skelton (8)
Yarm CP School, Yarm

The Legendary Ship, Titanic

She was the queen of the ocean
Finally she set off from Southampton
Bands playing, people singing.
The Titanic hit invisible ice, buried under the sea.
It took three to four hours for Titanic to finally sink.
The legendary ship, Titanic.

Thomas Cleasby (8)
Yarm CP School, Yarm

The Poem Of The Titanic

It's time to sail the Titanic over the Atlantic Ocean
As everybody knows there are icebergs in the sea
But nobody saw the iceberg and the ship crashed;
The worst that happened,
Seven hundred and five people died,
That was the end of the Titanic.

Christopher Brooks (8)
Yarm CP School, Yarm

The Hulk

Marvel at my strength, my power,
Fast, swift, twisting, turning,
I throw the cart round the track,
There's no place to hide,
I'm not on your side,
The green snake slaloming through the air,
I am the green goblin of terror.
Fierce, fast, frightening,
Hypnotising you evermore,
Scaring you till you drop to the floor,
Marvel comic,
I am supersonic,
My looks may be deceiving,
But you keep on retrieving,
The power you feel as you ride on me.

Luke Hobbs (10)
Yarm CP School, Yarm

My Special Home

(Inspired by 'Magic Box' by Kit Wright)

I will put in my home . . .
A pillow that smells like a flower,
A big trampoline to bounce on.

I will put in my home . . .
A big castle so I can play in it,
A rose to cover my room.

I will put in my home . . .
A big sweet that fills my house,
And my friend Arabella.

My house is made from bricks and flowers.
My family should be happy forever and ever.

Josie Barber (9)
Yarm CP School, Yarm

Titanic Disaster

Queen of the sea set sail,
Heading for New York,
She was brought down by ice.
Women and children first,
Sea was wild and icy.
Took four hours to sink,
Then sank down to a watery grave,
No more queen of the sea,
The ship was gone.
Titanic.

Joseph Davison (8)
Yarm CP School, Yarm

Disaster At Sea

Looking and panicking
Seeing jagged icebergs like Everest,
Explosive bangs all around.
People screaming and weeping,
Mind-numbing frost sweeping over me.
Distress flares screaming,
Splashes of suicidal people fading, fading.

Sean Jarvis (8)
Yarm CP School, Yarm

The Disaster

The bands were playing, everyone cheering.
Queen of the sea, unsinkable, colossal, towering over the ocean.
Looming towards her doom.
Colliding with a huge mountain of ice.
Floundering, sinking down into furious water.
The bands were playing, nobody's cheering.

Christopher Moorhouse (8)
Yarm CP School, Yarm

Titanic

Titanic crashing, gushing, exploding, banging,
Water whirling,
Passengers worried.
I can't believe what's going on,
I hate to look at petrified faces.
I have a deadly feeling as the freezing cold water
Like pins and needles crashes into my face.
Am I alive?
Please tell me, am I alive?

Rehman Khalid (8)
Yarm CP School, Yarm

Titanic!

Crash! Titanic hit the iceberg,
I put my hand on the floor, it was cold,
I feel as though I will never see the daylight again,
I'm going to drown,
I feel dizzy as the water touches me.
I'm in deadly panic,
I'm so scared, it feels like I'm not here, and then . . . I'm not.

Beth Foster (8)
Yarm CP School, Yarm

Titanic!

Titanic crashed!
Splash! Distressed people jumped overboard.
Iceberg like an island,
People screamed as I touched the window,
My hand went numb.
Explosive bang, the lights went out.
Silence all around . . .

Jenny Rookes (8)
Yarm CP School, Yarm

Disaster

The Titanic is going to go forever,
Splash! As all the lifeboats go down.
I feel dizzy as the ship tilts.
I am surrounded by screams.
I see something frightening, an iceberg!
I must get into a lifeboat,
No ship has come to save us.
I get onto a lifeboat; I'm too numb to move.
I look back as one of the funnels fall off and she's gone.
I feel so heartbroken.

Daphne Papaioannou (8)
Yarm CP School, Yarm

Titanic Poem

Cold bars,
Numbing hands,
Scared passengers screaming hysterically,
Frozen shiver went down my spine,
Deadly panic,
Explosive bang!
Heart stopping alarm fills the night,
Jagged iceberg, frozen oasis.

George McLeary (8)
Yarm CP School, Yarm

Titanic

I heard the iceberg crash.
People dived in horror.
People splashed in the freezing water.
Window freezing fast.

Lewis Brittain (8)
Yarm CP School, Yarm

The Spinning Teacup!

I am the swirling sound of softness,
On the saucer I spin.
Journey through the fantasies,
That you and I are in.
Boys and girls you have no fear,
As you will see
The ghost train is not here.
We want happy faces,
As we pick up the pace.
Round and round,
We don't hit the ground.
Spin and spin,
I see your grin.
Twirl and twirl,
Swirl and swirl.
Have fun.

Zara Metcalfe (10)
Yarm CP School, Yarm

Titanic's Disaster

A splash
A tear,
A fear of death,
Water at my feet,
So cold they burn.
I heard an explosive bang,
A tilt came, I desperately held onto the bar
I felt as if I was dead,
I almost jumped overboard.
I didn't want to suffer.

Joanna Knutsen (8)
Yarm CP School, Yarm

The Ghost Train!

Fright, shiver, doom!
Swaying on tracks,
I hypnotise you like a pendulum to come,
Unknown is the shock so scary,
My breath so smoky,
And the ghosts leaping and lurking.
The ride is hidden, forbidden to know,
Werewolf cries, a chamber of surprise,
Shaking, forcing out the truth,
Your real feelings overflow.
I am the ghoulish ghosts,
The daring devils,
The fearful Frankenstein.
Spook and terror pump through my heart,
Nightmares begin to start,
Kindness a fairy tale,
Fright reality.
Dismay, dread, terror!
Feel my fear, test your courage,
Ride on me, see my world,
The truth, my train,
The ghost train!

Jessica Thornton (10)
Yarm CP School, Yarm

The Big Wheel

My still skeleton stands proud in the sky
Arms reaching way up high,
Slow, then fast, high, then low
Jump on quick, off we go!
Rapid, quick, getting hard as we climb,
The top is our destiny, we will never stop.
The climb is slow but the drop is fast, flying through the air.
We climb again, my bulky body struggles before the sudden
Drop!

Abigail Watson (10)
Yarm CP School, Yarm

The Hulk

I come alive,
People clutching my straps,
Screaming with fright!
I pick up speed.
Come charging out,
So much power,
Diving down,
Jerking everyone,
I fly upside down,
Feel everyone's heart racing,
They pretend they aren't frightened,
People see me as
Bright green,
Bright purple,
The most powerful warrior!
In the shape of a swirling river,
The fastest,
Then . . .
. . . I halt to a stop.

Lottie Fletcher (10)
Yarm CP School, Yarm

Pirate Ship

I awake from the dead.
Chains clatter as I wait for my victim.
Swaying and swinging in a storm you will find me.
I move like the sea.
Nothing to hang on to.
Losing air, losing gravity as I swing higher.
I rock in the wind you can hear me creak.
I could fall down any second,
Argh!
I finally stop and wait for my next victim!

Laurel Robinson (10)
Yarm CP School, Yarm

Simulator

Used, sparkling, ready,
Surrounded by rides,
Big and bold - small and puny,
There is no better than me.
I trick you into my claws of doom,
Hypnotising, terrorising,
There is no escape,
I have you in my grasp,
I outwit the others.
My prey is coming, coming, coming,
As I close you in.
A rocket body, with cinemas insides,
Tank tracks for feet,
A truck head,
My body combines; I am the best of all things.
You take a risk going near me,
You better run away,
I will find you,
You are my next victim,
Watch out, be aware,
I'll get you,
My victims are thrilled by my miniature insides.
The others may be good,
But I am the best.
I am thrill,
I am speedy
I am risk,
I am suspense . . .
A sudden strike.

James Healey (10)
Yarm CP School, Yarm

Ghost Train

Between terror and giggles,
You will find me.
A séance of horror,
You spy on tonight.
I meet the bravest at night-time,
You laugh, giggle and smile
But I'll lure the victims in,
I'll take them on a dark, damp spin.
Eerie ride,
I am the master magician,
I am the eternal illusionist,
I petrify them,
Terrify them,
Make them run away!
I lurk around the snappy corners,
Then they draw back,
To make their escape.
As I refill my vial,
Drink in victims' screams,
I am still there,
When you turn out the light,
I dive into their dreams.

Jamie Fox (10)
Yarm CP School, Yarm

The Titanic Voyage

It was the biggest ship in the world
She was the queen of the sea.
It took four hours to sink
After she set off to sail to New York.
It sank in the Atlantic,
Lots of people died.

Alexia Thompson (8)
Yarm CP School, Yarm

The Magnum Force

As I await my victims to step upon my back,
I lie lazily on the great big track,
They climb on one by one,
With their friend to help them along,
What they don't know is what's lying ahead,
Will they have nightmares when they go to bed?

My twisty, turny, loopy rail,
Might remind you of the shell of a snail,
Because I'm moving really fast,
The rattling sound might not last,
My amazing colours are white and red,
'This is going to be wicked,' a little boy said.

Whizzing, twisting,
Screams are listing
Coming round the bend,
Here is the end!

Caroline Kelly (10)
Yarm CP School, Yarm

Bungee Jump

I wait so still and drift away to the land of nod,
Then suddenly, someone pulls my leg,
It's time to ride the bungee jump,
I'll give you butterflies in your tum,
People watch you hiccup then you spring up so high,
Soaring the world's sky,
Come see the world and float away to a different atmosphere,
Up high, down low, somersault I go,
Jump in, get strapped up,
The end is near,
The hiccup comes back,
Faces are red,
Exhaustion is revealed
End of journey.

Alice Kilburn (10)
Yarm CP School, Yarm

The Hulk

I am terrifying, smooth and loopy,
You wouldn't dare take a step on my back,
But I'm forcing you,
I will frighten you to your death,
I'm too fast for you,
I'm sure,
You're only a little girl to me,
I'm purple and green, too bright for you,
I'm too deadly for you,
Step on my back and off we go,
We twist, turn and zoom,
I can feel your hands tensing and gripping onto the seat,
I'll make you feel like you're going to fall off the edge,
I can see you screaming and shouting,
But I'm not going to stop!

James Bell (10)
Yarm CP School, Yarm

The Spritzer

Patiently I wait,
Silent and still,
My smile slowly spreads,
As I hear hesitant footsteps
Cautiously climbing towards me.
Off we go,
Swirling round as colours blur,
Dizziness strikes me in the eye,
Now we fly high in the sky,
All bright colours, pink, yellow and green.
I feel tummies churning around me,
Now we start to slow,
For the last time round we go.

Kelly Brittain (10)
Yarm CP School, Yarm

The Big Wheel

As midnight comes to a close,
Watching high in the sky,
A glinting light that shines so bright,
My twinkling, gleaming, blue eye.
My head is ready, I feel alive,
The time is ticking by,
I'm ready to go round and round,
I'm about to fly.
A creature creeping up the path,
Is heading straight my way,
They'll regret they came on me,
And dream about me everyday.
Humans chattering vigorously,
I'm going to twirl away,
The atmosphere is ready,
Creatures' heads will be spinning till May!
A steady start's coming slowly,
My neck touches the sky,
I'm ready to make you scream,
And I'm ready to make you cry.
Swishing, flicking, spinning,
Take-off, don't stop turning,
Dazzling, flying high,
Scary, stomach churning.
Looking down upon the floor,
Fun-seekers give money and cheer,
Big pink clouds are given out,
I think my next ride's near.
I'm the biggest and the best,
I'm master of this fair,
So take a whirling ride on me,
Though you're in for a great big scare!

Imogen Phillips (10)
Yarm CP School, Yarm

Big Wheel

This is me high in the sky, I await,
Looking for people to come, I'll scare my bait.
I whirl and twirl shaped as a curl, until I'm satisfied,
Want to get off, start to cough; now they wish they'd lied.
My carts are old and squeaky,
When people come off they're looking peaky.
Get to the top all of them gasp.
Get to the bottom they say, 'At last!'
I look all around
Coming safely to the ground.
Round and round I repeat,
'Have a go on me, take a seat.'
I hear people say, 'Not that again
You must be crazy, are you insane?'
Now how do you think that makes me feel?
I'm quite a big guy, only a wheel,
So I dare you to challenge me,
Look to the future, wait and see.

Robyn Maddison (10)
Yarm CP School, Yarm

The Spritzer

As my unexpecting victims climb on my legs
I am charging energy to swing and twirl.
Off we go,
As I set off I am really slow
I start to get faster and faster till my victims are screaming,
I still go faster and faster till my bones ache
But I still carry on,
I am swinging and twirling
I am brightly coloured and everybody notices.
My muscles are groaning and I conclude,
I linger for the next victims to appear.

Ross Mungin (10)
Yarm CP School, Yarm

Teacups

Everyone getting in, the
Bars are down, we're
All buckled in we're,
Ready to go!
We're turning faster,
Faster,
We're spinning,
Whirling,
We're spinning and turning,
I think I'm ready to burst,
But we're all still spinning,
Spinning,
We're slowing, slowing and,
Then a sudden creak,
We've stopped, the ride is over.

James Herbert (11) & Kieran Richardson (10)
Yarm CP School, Yarm

Shake It

I will scare you.
You will regret the day you came on
But jump aboard,
For some confusion.
Shaking, spinning, swirling around.
Screaming, shrieking, laughing sounds.
Are you frightened?
You should be terrified.
Do you want to stop?
Shaking, spinning, swirling, around,
Screaming, shrieking, laughing sounds.
My victims are getting tired,
It's time to slow down,
Until next time.

Karla Purvis (10)
Yarm CP School, Yarm

The Oblivion

As I stand motionless I wait for my riders
With the slightest body heat I awake and am settled to scare.
When people relax on my hands, my toes, my eyes and my nose,
I begin.
I set off slowly up the energetic ramp
Smoothly and steadily round the curl
I hang at the top and say my verse, 'Don't look down!'
I can smell fear, sense fear, feel fear!
In the quick of a blink I zoom out of control.
People feel mindless, obliviated and scream as hard as they can,
They're scared stiff and shaking.
I come out the other side.
As people come off slowly my job is done.
I can rest.

Lauren Wallace (10)
Yarm CP School, Yarm

Rolling Dice Ride

My deathly face awaiting and watching.
Creak, creak of my victims' feet on silver metal steps.
They better beware of my spin and speed,
The speed of dice rolling on a snake eyes board.
Voices screaming in my three ears,
I am building up a tornado, faces turn green.
My master is waiting to blast up the gas,
I reverse to slow down with a loud squeal.
Back to a tornado, everyone screaming,
I finally stop, my master unlocks everyone.
Jelly legs wobble my metal.

James Edward Hunt (10)
Yarm CP School, Yarm

Spritzer!

I shudder slightly as my first victim steps on board,
Confused, nervous faces make me grin
My thriller ride is ready
Slowly
I start
Swaying to swishing
Swishing to rolling
Then we're off at full speed
Screaming and screeching fills the air
Hurtling round and round
Rising, falling,
Dropping and whirling
Throwing people from their seats
Faces grow paler
The dazzling sight of the bright, jazzy lights
As confusion sets in
When will it end?
It comes to a final drop,
Dipping round,
Petrified faces become . . .
Relieved.

Amy Barrett (10)
Yarm CP School, Yarm

Titanic

New York voyage
She was the biggest ship in the world.
She set off from Southampton.
She was the queen of the sea!
In the distance there was a big chunk of ice.
Suddenly an iceberg!
It took four hours to sink.
Lots of people died when its voyage to New York ended.

Hayley Malcolm (8)
Yarm CP School, Yarm

My House
(Inspired by 'Magic Box' by Kit Wright)

I will put in my home . . .
Forgiveness to brighten up Henry's life.

I will put in my home . . .
Some happiness to make colour on 131 Ballyentyre Road.

I will put in my home . . .
A happy and forgiving mum who is a celebrity.

I will put in my home . . .
A scrumptious piece of everlasting chocolate.

My home is made from . . .
Double-glazed chocolate windows
With a roof made from caramel tiles.
The lights are made from extra white chocolate.

Alexander Nargol (9)
Yarm CP School, Yarm

The Water Ride!

My carriers bob patiently waiting to begin their bumpy journey,
The fun-seekers climb in,
Laughing giggling and shouting with joy,
Are they aware of the shock they face?
As the ride begins their stomachs can't face the jerky ride anymore,
So they scream and shout but my owner's not about.
I make the ride faster and everybody screams, 'No!'
But I don't stop the ride because I'm having so much fun
And there's lots more fun that hasn't been done.
I let them off,
Are they prepared for the drop?

Kimberley Foster (11)
Yarm CP School, Yarm

Tragedy Ship

They said the Titanic was queen of the sea,
And everyone else believed them.
They also said it was unsinkable,
People believed that as well.
It set sail at Southampton and wanted to go to New York.
The Titanic was so massive it was the biggest in the world
And when it hit the iceberg twelve hundred and sixty-nine
                                             people died.
The Carpathia tried to save the day, it saved seven hundred and five.
The iceberg hit it on the starboard side,
Making a three hundred foot gap.
All the people panicked and ran around the deck.
When it finally sunk they were in a watery grave.

William Levitt (8)
Yarm CP School, Yarm

The Grasshopper

The cling clang of my paying victims startles me,
I shiver when my prey tickle my arms,
My unwary victims are ready to do battle,
But they'll come off with a bit of a rattle,
We are whizzing off into the distance,
Up and down we fly around,
Have they had enough?
I come to an end,
Their faces are red,
They'll have to cope,
With a spinning head.

Alistair Aitken (10)
Yarm CP School, Yarm

The Dodgems

As I wait, I recharge for the crashes,
The music is playing as people climb on my back,
The sharp turns will whizz them out their seats,
The crashes will yank them back,
Are they ready for the ride?
The familiar bell rings, it's time to go,
Crashing,
Bashing together,
Turning
Churning in the arena,
Hurling
Bursting my victims
Loud
A rough ride,
Bashing
Battering my cars
But the ride will go on
The excitement grows
The laughing is louder
I will not stop
I will never
Stop!

Hannah Sayer (10)
Yarm CP School, Yarm

Watery Titanic

The queen of the sea, Titanic
Southampton she set sail
She hit ice at 12pm
It was all in panic
The starboard side was in danger
Now she's in a watery grave
The legendary Titanic.

Helen Probert (8)
Yarm CP School, Yarm

The Waltzer's Poem!

You will find me
Spinning and twirling
In the dark,
Fiercely whizzing my passengers
Around and around.
I am fast!
I am furious!
I am ready to go!
I hypnotize you all
Into a scary,
Pitch-black whirl.
My lights flash,
My music blasts,
Power and violence
Are my main sources!
I am lively,
Energetic, loud,
And high powered.
I am a rough ride
Along a wavy path.
I start to fade . . .
And slow down gently.
My passengers come off me dizzy but amused.

Evie Thompson (10)
Yarm CP School, Yarm

Titanic Disaster

Queen of the sea set sail,
Brought down by shadowy ice,
Sank in the icy sea.
Carpathia set sail for rescue
Women and children first.
Down to the icy grave.

Emily Rankin (8)
Yarm CP School, Yarm

Titanic

Explosive
Bang!
Plates crash to the ground,
As the moving mountain tears a hole out of Titanic's side.
Water comes gushing in.
The great ship is sinking!
Screams can be heard for miles around.
I stop in my tracks as the monster breaks the ship in two.
The falling ice from the mountain crashes onto the ship.
People are diving into the water.
I jump, I feel the cold all around me - so cold it hurts!
I see lifeboats rowing away, the great ship is gone.
We are left alone!

Ellie Bourner (8)
Yarm CP School, Yarm

A Home For Happiness

(Inspired by 'Magic Box' by Kit Wright)

I will put in my house . . .
The sound of happiness
The laughs of happy children
And a gateway to a place to watch the sunset
Over the dazzling, clear water.

I will put in my home . . .
The top of the highest hill listening to the rainforest
Where there is always the taste of chocolate in your mouth.

I will put the sound of love, care and the most amazing tree
That shall find your love and makes you smile.

Rowan Bliss (9)
Yarm CP School, Yarm

A Home For Happiness

(Inspired by 'Magic Box' by Kit Wright)

I will put in my house . . .
The sound of a tropical rainforest.
The clear blue water coming out of an elephant's trunk.
The feel of Maltesers melting in your mouth.

I will put in my house . . .
The love from all living creatures.
A magic time clock that will stand straight as a giraffe.
A magic garden with the comfiest bed in the world.

My home is made from . . .
A mother's gold and silver and the rest from everlasting chocolate
And the door hinges from flower petals.

I shall swim with dolphins and watch them jumping.

Charlotte Cooney (9)
Yarm CP School, Yarm

The Magic Home

(Inspired by 'Magic Box' by Kit Wright)

I will put in my home . . .
A train set to play with all day.
A remote control car to speed around this home.
A football to play fantastic football with Wayne Rooney.

I will put in my home . . .
My best friends in the world.
A kitten to cuddle that's ginger and white and fluffy.

My home is made from chocolate sweets and ice cream
And it's made from biscuit as well.

I shall have a party in my home,
It is a really nice time at my home.

Curtis Mackay (10)
Yarm CP School, Yarm

My Magical Warm Home

(Inspired by 'Magic Box' by Kit Wright)

I will put in my home . . .
A lovely silky sofa that turns into a magical rainforest
A gorgeous comfy water bed that wobbles like a water fountain,
And a lovely big garden that has trickling water that is magic
When you turn it on, the smooth round button lighting up.

I will put in my home . . .
The finest sound to put me to sleep every night,
The first sound of a jacuzzi bubbling up
Overflowing with secrets of joy.

I will put in my home . . .
A gorgeous cosy study room
So I could play on my computer all day and do my homework.

I will put in my home . . .
The finest chocolate that ever lasts
So we could eat it and it will still be there
And I could have a giant fun play area all for me
And I would play on it every night and every day.

My home is made from . . .
Rich gold that dazzles in the moonlight.

I shall sleep and listen to the gorgeous rainforest in my home.

Sally Leishman (9)
Yarm CP School, Yarm

The Queen Of The Sea

Titanic was the biggest ship in the world
Heading for New York
Tragedy struck in the icy seas
People panicked! Women and children in the lifeboats first
Into the icy graves they drift
Survivors, not many
Queen of the sea sunk,
Never to be seen again.

Joseph Rodgers (8)
Yarm CP School, Yarm

My Hopeful Home

(Inspired by 'Magic Box' by Kit Wright)

I will put in my home . . .
The bluest swimming pool
With three dolphins leaping from its sky-reflecting waters.
A selection of waterfalls to put in a secret garden.
The most beautiful crystal ball in which I can see the future.

I will put in my home . . .
A golden love tree
The most magical container that makes everyday exciting for Henry.
A clock that will stop, rewind and fast forward time as I wish.

I will put in my home . . .
A photo of Henry's mum and dad.
A friend that Henry could play with.
A good pot overflowing with joy.

I will put in my home . . .
A secret pot full of food.
An overflowing pot of money.
The best clothes ever.
With a minty flavoured bubblegum house
And I shall have love in my house.

Sophie Bell (9)
Yarm CP School, Yarm

Tragedy Ship

She was the biggest ship
Heading for New York
Sailing through icy waters
People panic from deck to deck
Iceberg fooled the crew
Lots of people died
Legendary ship, Titanic.

Matthew Healey (8)
Yarm CP School, Yarm

Dodgem

Bruising, bashing, battering,
They are thumping and clattering,
Between a grin and a fright,
Between a shriek and a cry,
Like a missile colliding,
Targeting others,
For in my arena,
Only the winners belong,
My eyes glare with rage,
I'm waiting for you,
In this bright place,
I will draw you into my space,
Ride on me and you will see,
The shiver of fright,
I am the dread of fear,
I am the lord of horror.

Jack Chapman (10)
Yarm CP School, Yarm

The Pirate Ship

Between a rise and a drop,
You will find me.

Rocking faster and higher
Through the day.

I sway pirates so high,
They scream fearing they will fall out.

I flow with the wind,
This way and that.

Board on me and help me find,
The treasure that I seek!

Eloise Crofts (10)
Yarm CP School, Yarm

The Big Ghost Wheel

The courage of people is satisfying,
Going so close to death,
People come off me screaming,
Some don't ever come off!
The souls of human creatures,
Still in torture!
I'm funny at the start,
But then at the end,
The creatures begin the torture,
You might never see light again,
For the people that dare,
Come on, come on, there are places available,
For the death of your lives,
Good death, happy death, sad death
Terrible death
Death
Death
Death is awaiting!

Alexander Murray (10)
Yarm CP School, Yarm

The Waltzers

Dizzy, dazed, disorientated.
You get on me nervously ready for a spin.
In the dark I wait for new daredevils to take for a spin.
I move like the fastest spinning top, swiftly and deadly.

I will take you for the ultimate spin,
Are you seeking a thrill or a scare?
Either way you'll get the best of the fair!

In the dark I'm a daredevil catcher,
With my thumping music and blazing lights
I lure them into my swirling madness.

Luke Bourner (10)
Yarm CP School, Yarm

The Bumper Car

Dark arrives,
Stars appear,
Bringing the next game,
The next contest,
Fear is creeping around me,
Like an invisible cloak,
Bashing music,
Battering my brain!
Flashing lights,
Hypnotising me,
Crowds appear,
For me, the ride of the night,
I move fast and serious!
Smoke is flying behind me,
I am weak but have strength,
From the world around me,
When I am hit I want payback,
I am there for a game,
I was made to ride,
There are flashes of movement,
From speed and fright,
Laughter can be a tear,
I want a fight,
I am bruised and battered,
But there, there for glory,
You need strength to survive.

Amélie Cowan (10)
Yarm CP School, Yarm

Titanic

There's an iceberg next to me.
Bangs, frightening smashes I can hear,
I cannot open my eyes, water is all over me, it's ghostly,
The sight, I cannot take my eyes off the ship.

Sean Brown (8)
Yarm CP School, Yarm

The Grave Of The Titanic

She was the queen of the sea, cheering when she left.
Smashed into ice that nobody could see.
Four hours to sink, unsinkable they thought.
But underestimated by ice
Women and children first, crew ordered.
Too much in panic
Nothing could stop such vicious rapids.
Which sent her to a watery grave.

Adam Herbert (8)
Yarm CP School, Yarm

The Unsinkable Ship

She was the unsinkable ship
Brought down by an iceberg.
The ship filled up with icy water,
Women and children on lifeboats first,
Even with the gash it took four hours to sink.
Carpathia saved seven hundred and five.
That's the poem of the Titanic.

Harry Spencer (8)
Yarm CP School, Yarm

Legend Of The Titanic

She sailed to New York
Which was her maiden voyage.
Titanic was the grandest, biggest ship on earth.
Took four hours to sink
It was all in a panic
Carpathia came to help
The legend of Titanic.

Oliver Dryden (8)
Yarm CP School, Yarm

Pony Express

I was just born yesterday
The 28th of bubbly May,
Me and my friend tickle babies toes,
The children want to come on me,
Because the ghost train loves big, black crows.
I'm the young, pretty, pony express,
My pony made riders think I'm a success!
Don't think that I'm a lonely stray,
Because I'm the pony express
And I'm here to stay!

Josephine Welsh (10)
Yarm CP School, Yarm

Tragedy Ship

The Titanic was the greatest ship of all,
It was huge and expensive, and very, very, very tall.
They thought it was unsinkable,
But it was proved very wrong, when a huge iceberg hit the hull.
People tried to flee, by getting into the lifeboats,
And rowing them into the sea.
Lots of people died that night, for they were in a great panic.
That was the end, the very, very end of the great, great Titanic.

Jacob Stokes (8)
Yarm CP School, Yarm

Queen Of The Sea

She was the queen of the sea.
Sunk with an iceberg.
The Carpathia came to help, saved seven hundred and five people.
Lots died.
It will never sail again.
It is still in its watery grave.

Matthew Nargol (8)
Yarm CP School, Yarm

The Freaky House

People see me and they don't want to see me again.
My best friend is Ghost Train.
It's because we are brought up to hurt and scare people.
All of the other rides hate us.
It's because they are soft.
If they want to be like that they can
We'll be tough!

We move fast, ducking and spinning,
That's the way we want to be.
Demolishing people's moods with the sheer speed.
We will twist and turn you into whinging wimps.
We'll swing you around, you will look like a chimp
Then we'll move you like a rocket zooming from the moon.
Then when you leave us, all you'll remember is our tune
You'll never come back, you'll never dare.
Try us at your peril because we don't care.

Jason Barnes (10)
Yarm CP School, Yarm

Magnum Force

I am fear - the ride black,
As I spin you around the twisted track!
Negative Gs push you back in your seat.
My twists and turns boost your heartbeat.
After a loop you don't feel whole,
After the ride, your stomach I've stole.
I am black,
I am fear,
I am screams,
Big, blue, bright, brilliant,
The end of the day draws near,
I rise once more, pulled by a gear,
Now I settle down, as lively as I may seem.
But I'll be ready tomorrow to be just as mean!

Tom Elliott (10)
Yarm CP School, Yarm

Waltzers

Scary, snazzy, safe,
I wait to start,
Waiting for people to come,
Suddenly people mount on
They ride me with a shiver,
They ride me with a quiver.
The metal bar slams down,
Crash on your lap.
My eyes start flashing,
A puff of my smoke,
Waiting and waiting to go,
The banging music decides to start,
Then I know I'm allowed to go,
My colourful colours make people really scared,
Hold on tight, we're ready, let's go!
Twisting, turning, round and round,
Then I go up and down.
Slow - steady - fast as I can go!
Soon we're whizzing round,
Chunky smoke smashing into your face!
Flashing lights come out to play,
Dancing around throughout the day,
My excitement slowly slips down,
Now I'm not as playful as you found,
Then I'm still . . .
Not moving . . .
Stood on my own . . .
Then I start again,
For the next person to go.

Bethany Gray (11)
Yarm CP School, Yarm

Space Mountain!

Dark, daunty, doom!
I wait for my passengers,
Shuffling along the track,
Crick
Crack
Crick
Crack
Entering total darkness,
As we fly into space,
I'll twist and turn,
Loop and swoop,
Hearing fatal cries and screams,
I move rapidly,
Suddenly turning corners -
Accelerating faster and faster,
Exploding with energy!
We zoom along at the speed of an erupting volcano,
All I see are people sharply jerking from side to side.
We are whizzing so swiftly along the track you can see stars,
Sick - tired - dizzy!

Lauren Jackson (11)
Yarm CP School, Yarm

The Dodgems

Bashing and crashing, zooming, exciting
That's the dodgems by me,
You feel the urge to ride and win
The contest the champion of the stage,
The people like me they have fun bashing and slicing
The other rides are jealous 'cause they like me the most.
Other rides say it's not fair, it's not my fault that I'm the best.
I don't like power down, the kids are so unhappy ,
Tomorrow they'll come again and have so much fun,
Tomorrow starts, power on . . .
Zooming round, so much fun slamming and crashing again.

Oliver Campbell (10)
Yarm CP School, Yarm

The Ghost Train

Creaking and groaning as I go along,
Murky grey, muddy brown and blood-drooling red
Are the colours I wear,
I am the demon of horridness,
I manage an evil smile
As those happy faces crumble to a wail of despair.

My ride is jerky and bumpy
So that those happy faces change,
I bump and cackle as I creep along,
Thick cotton spiderwebs dangle over your heads,
High-pitched screams fill your ears on my ride,
Creeping, lurking as I turn the side,
You'll decide you hate my ride,
Biting things snap in the air,
Be ready . . .
Because you're in for a scare!

Siân Gers (10)
Yarm CP School, Yarm

Ghost Train

My body was created a few years ago,
But my spirit has been in this world for centuries.
I look quite scary but that is not true,
I am very scary indeed that I say to you.
I am:
The scare in scary,
The creep in creepy,
The horror in horrific.
My skin is stretched tight across my flesh,
My back is broken so therefore I cannot stand straight.

In my domain frightened children hug their mothers,
Because of my loyal companions.
Yes, I am a ride called a ghost train,
Ride me and you will go insane.

Tim Spencer (10)
Yarm CP School, Yarm

The Ghost Train

Behind the wimpy tea cups
In the dark misty night
People queue up for the scare of their life.

For through those old rotting doors
And up that round rickety ramp
They won't know what's hit them!

You think you're so brave
As you wait your turn
As little children clamber off
As pale as the moon.

I slither silently down to the
Dark dangerous dungeon
Where all but one scurrying rat
Is yet to be seen.

As you sit in your seat
Ready to go, last minute
Moments begin to slow.

You think you can beat me
But really you can't,
No one can.

As I force you off
One of my many carriages,
You're thinking I'll never come back,
I'll never dare.

The ghost train's my name
Scaring children is my game.

Emily Hadlow (10)
Yarm CP School, Yarm

Roller Coaster

I am the wig taker,
I am the laugher,
I'd drain away your strength,
And corkscrew your mind,
I'll blow you away with my G force wrath,
Batter,
Bang,
Bone crushing,
And disorientate your body
I'll kill your mind,
I'll make you die,
Another victim dead and gone,
The body will be eaten by the metal,
The weak forgotten,
Forever lost.

Benjamin Andrews (10)
Yarm CP School, Yarm

Whizzing Action

If you do not ride me,
Your life would be so grumpy.
Look at me whizzing past,
Think what you are missing.

Look at me, I'm so fast,
Look at me really go,
Oooh you can think so,
But when you come off me,
Don't blame me when you're sick!

You'll think back on your life,
When I slip side to side.
When I jerk you up you will go,
Into another dimension.

Jonathan Colclough (10)
Yarm CP School, Yarm

The Bomber

At the beginning of the fair I stand there all alone,
When you see me I don't look frightening,
But when you get on me,
You'll think I'm scary,
If you think you won't get a fright,
Jump on me and have a ride.

When you get on me you will know,
Just how loud you have to shriek and shout,
When I swish, sway and spin,
You will know to listen to me.

I will spin round and round,
I will teach you how to learn,
I will teach you to be mysterious,
I will make you have a nightmare.

Other rides can't compare with me,
I'm the master of the world,
If you think you aren't scared,
Come on me and then you'll be taught.

Sophie Cullum (10)
Yarm CP School, Yarm

Roller Coaster

Between all those boring rides you'll find a super speedy,
It's the whizzing roller coaster, not a ride that's weedy.

As I twist and turn along following my energetic track,
I love to do the loopedy loop once, twice or more
I hope it won't break your back.

The people who ride are certain to find the best ride they ever saw,
All the people that have been on the ride will want to go on
more and more!

James Heavers (10)
Yarm CP School, Yarm

Roller Coaster

Speeding, skidding down the track,
Soon you will hope you were back,
Whizzing, screaming, being sick,
As the cart goes clickety-click.

Shouting as we go through the loop,
Sprinting as the waiting people whoop!
Dizzy people on the track,
Now you wish you were back.

Stopping at the top of a really steep hill,
At night you'll have to take a sleeping pill,
Rattling down the hill, we're going very fast,
This go will be your very, very last,
Screaming, scratching is all I can hear,
I don't even have to steer!

James Harkin (10)
Yarm CP School, Yarm

The Big Wheel

I whirl, spin and whizz all day,
I'm the happy one, you'll like me,
The speed I go is lightning,
Fire spitting out,
The screams come when you're stuck at the top
All so high,
I'm the king of happiness.
Smiles when you leave,
When you come off
I see smiles,
People trying to get on again
I do hope people come back
So I can carry them again.

Harry Robinson (10)
Yarm CP School, Yarm

Ghost Train

You think you're so brave,
As soon as you jump on me you are afraid,
I hypnotise you,
The unwary victims,
I am a devil dressed in black,
I am Satan as I pull you on the track.

They call me evil,
A grumpy old man,
All crooked and torn,
Well if that's who I am,
Then they are all marshmallows, all pink and soft,
Giggly and girlie as soft as a mouse.

You'll always find me in a dark corner,
I'll catch your eye with my gothic ways,
The other rides just make you smile,
I'll be the one who is worthwhile.

After the ride you'll be so scared,
You'll wish you never dared,
I'll leave you with a nightmare or two,
As a present from me to you,
Take the challenge, ride again,
I don't care because I'm a ghost train.

Samantha Wilkin (10)
Yarm CP School, Yarm

Titanic

The Titanic is sinking,
The iceberg is crashing,
People shouting, 'Help!'
I can see people diving into the frozen Atlantic Ocean with a splash,
A mass of scared faces all around me.
I could not hear anything but crash! Crash! Crash!

Thomas Mullen (8)
Yarm CP School, Yarm

The Magic House

(Inspired by 'Magic Box' by Kit Wright)

I'll put in my home . . .
A secret garden to smell the beautiful flowers
Some everlasting chocolate to continuously eat
A television which shows only my favourite programmes.

I'll put in my home . . .
A crystal water swimming pool to swim and swim
The gorgeous taste of butter on toast
A nice comfy bed and diamond walls.

My home is made from . . .
Chocolate and diamonds
With a sky picture of silver stars
And a big silver moon on the roof.

I shall play and party in my house
And have the most wonderful time.

Joseph Smith (9)
Yarm CP School, Yarm

The Big Wheel

I'm a happy, jolly ride that will make you laugh and scream.
I sway side to side as I let people off and pick them up.
The big wheel excites you when I spin you around and around twisting
and turning to make you squeal and laugh.
I like to make people laugh and giggle.
My best friend is the slide of joy.
I get along good with other rides
And they get along good with me too.
I always make sure that people feel happy and great after the ride.
I show you the rest of the people below
Some tiring and some nice and jolly.

Sophie Hayes (10)
Yarm CP School, Yarm

The Slide Of Joy

I am the sweet wonder of life.
The children that ride me
Come off with loads of laughs and smiles.
The slide of fun is what I am.
I love to see people having a great time with their family and friends.
But if you ride me you will dream about a land of fantasies
With a pot of gold at the other end of a rainbow.
You're near the end, but there is still more.
The sun shines when someone is on me,
That makes them so much happier.
If you're sad or mad come on me and you will be glad.
You see the end around the bend,
Bump! You have hit the floor surface.
'Mum, can I go again?'
You say in a cheerful way.
'Yes of course you can,' she says
The journey starts again, and you're off!

Lucia Harrison (10)
Yarm CP School, Yarm

The Log Flume

I am a swirling ball of fun a never-ending dream,
My favourite ride, a big water ball of fun,
As I slide through the day having bundles of joy,
By the time your go is finished you will never want to get off me.

As I creak slowly down the track getting faster and faster
Watching my back with a never-ending crack, crack, crack
As I slither down the track of course
I'm watching my back as I storm down the track
Then going all the way back, tired as I am, I carry on through the day.

When the day is finally over it's time to rest my rusty, old wheel
For tomorrow is another day, time to play, play, play all day.

Charlotte Burguiere (10)
Yarm CP School, Yarm

The Merry-Go-Round

When my handle is turned
I wave my wand and the magic begins.
You forget all your fears
And dry your tears,
Happiness will reign.

Smoothly spinning,
Fun 'n' funky,
Vibrant colours,
Snazzy 'n' snappy.

Slowly I stop,
No more music.
The spell ends as everyone gets off,
Spellbound and inspired.
More people get on,
And I wave my wand,
Again, again and again . . .

Lydia Papaioannou (10)
Yarm CP School, Yarm

The Sweetie House

(Inspired by 'Magic Box' by Kit Wright)

I will put in my house . . .
A flying pig made of pink chocolate
A chocolate television that shows only chocolate programmes
A sugar lump bed with a marshmallow mattress.

I will put in my house . . .
A tub full of chocolate butter to put on my toast
A marshmallow in every cup of tea
A view to see the half-eaten white chocolate moon.

Rachel Kitson (9)
Yarm CP School, Yarm

Roller Coaster

Whizzing, screaming in shock,
As you go down my side,
Hoping that the seat restraints,
Will hold you when you glide.

I am a near death experience,
Unlike those babies' toys,
Hearing people screaming,
Is a lovely, gentle noise.

If you think you're tough enough,
You'll have to try my track,
Hopefully I've scared you,
So you won't be coming back.

I like my G force to be a powerful weapon,
Stabbing into their fear like knives
My aim is to make people scream,
Shout for their lives.

David Elliott (10)
Yarm CP School, Yarm

The Big Wheel

You have a jolly ride, moving slowly round and round,
The big wheel, me,
Likes to make little skipping children happy, going up and down.
Stopping at the top seeing all the sights,
Moving round and round all through the nights.
Feeling all excited waiting in line,
Watching all the people up on that ride!
Once you get up there, searching down below
Enjoying stopping up in the cloudy sky.
Taking some photos of all the fairground rides,
Enjoying your only night on all of those rides!

Rebecca Simpson (10)
Yarm CP School, Yarm

My Magic House

(Inspired by 'Magic Box' by Kit Wright)

I will put in my home . . .
A giant football pitch
A football player that's rich
A servant that does everything.

I will put in my home . . .
A Christmas Day in my living room
A giant chair that acts like a fire
A space that you don't have to fly to.

I will put in my home . . .
The richest man in the world
A private jet that you don't have to fly to
A big, big bouncy castle.

I will put in my home . . .
A door that opens up to Heaven
A place where I can go to when I'm sad
A person that makes you laugh.

My home is made from the grass of Wembley
The skin of a cat and
The silk of a baby's blanket.

I shall play on the football pitch
I will bounce on the bouncy castle until my feet get tired
I will go to Heaven and bounce on the clouds.

Michael Taylor (9)
Yarm CP School, Yarm

Titanic

I heard a bang! What was it?
Was it a ship hitting us or was it a bomb?
No, it was an iceberg!
It couldn't be.
Yes, it was a moving mountain, white like milk.
On the bottom like a cola Slush Puppy all rotting.

Jack Close (8)
Yarm CP School, Yarm

Henry's Enchanted Home

(Inspired by 'Magic Box' by Kit Wright)

I will put in my house . . .
My loving parents who love me to bits
A nice piano to play all day
A colossal TV with gazillions of channels.

I will put in my house . . .
A gigantic pool as big as Everest
A massive helicopter to see the world
A sea to swim with dolphins in.

I will put in my house . . .
A massive bedroom with an extra springy bed
A bunch of friends to play and share with
And everything proof shielded so no one can get in.

I will put in my house . . .
A pet cat to keep me company
A money tree in my own garden so I never run out of cash
An invisible car to drive round town.

My home is made of everlasting chocolate fudge and love
And in my home I shall party and play.

Ben Watson (9)
Yarm CP School, Yarm

The Great Titanic

Loud shouts, scared faces.
Gushing water, plates crashing.
An explosive bang, a moving mountain,
Frozen windows, cold bars.
Frantic splashes, heart-stopping screams.
Distressed passengers, panicking wildly.
That's what I saw, that's what I heard,
That's what I touched, that's what I felt like
On the great Titanic, on the 14th April 1912.

Toby Chapman (8)
Yarm CP School, Yarm

The Wishing House

(Inspired by 'Magic Box' by Kit Wright)

I will put in my home . . .
The sound and cry of a rainforest
And the calm atmosphere where all nature is happy in
your command,

And a sun that shines all day
And a gate of excited children.

I will put in my house . . .
A silk hammock with famous singers to lullaby you,
An image of your family if they have passed,
Friends to sleep with at sleepovers,
And sweets if wanted.

I will put in my home . . .
A funhouse for you to play in with ever-changing surprises,
A cooked roast meal and large breakfasts,
A white horse to give rides, picnics with chocolate and pop.

I will put in my home . . .
A games field for rounders and football and much more,
A reading corner for when tired and bored
A PC and TV with games channels
A swimming pool to swim with dolphins, to relax.

My house is made of glass that never smashes, to see the world,
And nature, with a gate leading to dreams where it will all
come true
And a waterfall spilling out from emerald trees.

My house is special because my family comes
And where friends come to play and surprise is all around ,
But I am not spoilt.

Imogen Byrne (10)
Yarm CP School, Yarm